First World War
and Army of Occupation
War Diary
France, Belgium and Germany

21 DIVISION
63 Infantry Brigade
Lincolnshire Regiment
8th Battalion
10 September 1915 - 31 July 1916

WO95/2158/1

The Naval & Military Press Ltd
www.nmarchive.com
Published in association with The National Archives

Published by

The Naval & Military Press Ltd

Unit 10 Ridgewood Industrial Park,
Uckfield, East Sussex,
TN22 5QE England
Tel: +44 (0) 1825 749494

www.naval-military-press.com

www.nmarchive.com

This diary has been reprinted in facsimile from the original. Any imperfections are inevitably reproduced and the quality may fall short of modern type and cartographic standards.

© **Crown Copyright**
Images reproduced by permission of The National Archives, London, England, 2015.

Contents

Document type	Place/Title	Date From	Date To
Heading	WO95/2158/1		
Heading	21st Division 63rd Infy Bde 8th Bn Lincolns. Regt Sep 1915-Jly 1916. To 37 Div 63 Bde		
Heading	63rd Inf. Bde. 21st Div. Battn. disembarked Boulogne from England 11.9.15. War Diary 8th Battn. The Lincolnshire Regiment. September (10.9.15-29.9.15) 1915 Attached : Appendix I.		
War Diary	Witley Camp	10/09/1915	10/09/1915
War Diary	Boulogne	11/09/1915	11/09/1915
War Diary	Bayenghem	13/09/1915	14/09/1915
War Diary	Racquinghem	20/09/1915	20/09/1915
War Diary	Norrent.	21/09/1915	21/09/1915
War Diary	Cauchy A La Tour	22/09/1915	22/09/1915
War Diary	Fours-a-Chaux	24/09/1915	25/09/1915
War Diary	Vermelles	25/09/1915	28/09/1915
War Diary	Linghem	29/09/1915	29/09/1915
Heading	Appendix I.		
Miscellaneous	A Form. Messages And Signals.		
Miscellaneous	Appendix I Action Near Loos 25-27 Sept. 1915	25/09/1915	25/09/1915
Miscellaneous	Notes On 8th (S) Battn. Lincolnshire Regiment by Captain F. Brown.		
Heading	21st Division 8th Lincolns Part of Vol I Oct 15 12/7595		
War Diary	Linghem	01/10/1915	01/10/1915
War Diary	Steenbecque	02/10/1915	02/10/1915
War Diary	Borre	06/10/1915	13/10/1915
War Diary	Strazeele	15/10/1915	24/10/1915
War Diary	Armentieres	26/10/1915	31/10/1915
Miscellaneous	8th (Serv) Bn Lincolnshire Regiment Roll of Officers by Companies. Appendix 2 Officers.	31/10/1915	31/10/1915
Heading	21st Division 8th Lincolns Vol:2 Nov.15 121/7621		
War Diary	Armentieres	01/11/1915	30/11/1915
Map	Map of Trenches 67 To 69. Appendix 2		
Miscellaneous	Roll Of Officers By Companies. Appendix III.	01/12/1915	01/12/1915
Heading	21st Div December 1915 8th Lincolns Vol:3 December 1915 121/7935		
War Diary	Armentieres	01/12/1915	31/12/1915
Miscellaneous	List of Casualties during month of Dec 1915	31/12/1915	31/12/1915
Miscellaneous	List of Reinforcements arrived during the month of December 1915	31/12/1915	31/12/1915
Heading	8th Lincolns. Vol:4 Jan 16 21/63 21		
War Diary	Armentieres	01/01/1916	31/01/1916
Miscellaneous	Roll Of Officers 8th Bn Lincolnshire Regt		
Miscellaneous	Casualties issued During The Month of January 1916	31/01/1916	31/01/1916
Heading	8th Lincolns Feb 1916 6 V		
Miscellaneous	Nominal Roll Of Officers 8th Bn Lincolnshire Rgt. 1 March 1916	01/03/1916	01/03/1916
War Diary	Armentieres	01/02/1916	29/02/1916
Miscellaneous	8th (Serv) Bn Lincolnshire Regt Reinforcements Arrived during the month of February 1916	01/03/1916	01/03/1916

Miscellaneous	8th (Service) The Lincolnshire Regiment Casualties For The Month of February 1916	01/03/1916	01/03/1916
War Diary	Armentieres	01/03/1916	31/03/1916
Miscellaneous	Roll Of Officers In 8th Bn Lincolnshire Regt.	29/03/1916	29/03/1916
Operation(al) Order(s)	Operation Orders No. 25 By Lieut Col R.H. Johnston D.S.O. Commanding Batt Lincolnshire Regiment Thursday 30th March 1916 Appendix IV	30/03/1916	30/03/1916
Heading	8 Lincolns Vol 7		
Miscellaneous	Nominal Roll of Officers serving with Unit 30th April 1916	30/04/1916	30/04/1916
War Diary	Longeau Allonville	01/04/1916	08/04/1916
War Diary	Buirre	08/04/1916	14/04/1916
War Diary	Meaulte	15/04/1916	22/04/1916
War Diary	La Neuville	22/04/1916	30/04/1916
Operation(al) Order(s)	Operation Order No 26 by Lieut Col R.H. Johnston D.S.O. Commanding 8th (S) Bn Lincolnshire Regt Thursday April 6th 1916	06/04/1916	06/04/1916
Operation(al) Order(s)	Operation Orders By Lieut Col R.H. Johnston D.S.O. Commanding 8th Bn Lincolnshire Regiment. Thursday 13th April 1916	13/04/1916	13/04/1916
War Diary	La Neuville	01/05/1916	02/05/1916
War Diary	Meaulte	03/05/1916	22/05/1916
War Diary	Ville	23/05/1916	23/05/1916
War Diary	La Neuville	24/05/1916	31/05/1916
Miscellaneous	8th Bn. Lincolnshire Regiment Programme of Worth Appendix 5		
Operation(al) Order(s)	Operation Orders No 38 By Major H. Pattinson Commdg. 8th Lincolnshire Regiment. Wednesday. 31st. May, 1916. Appendix 6	31/05/1916	31/05/1916
Miscellaneous	A Form. Messages And Signals.		
War Diary	La Neuville	01/06/1916	01/06/1916
War Diary	Bois Des Tailles.	01/06/1916	11/06/1916
War Diary	Meaulte	12/06/1916	20/06/1916
War Diary	La Neuville	21/06/1916	27/06/1916
War Diary	Ville.	28/06/1916	30/06/1916
Heading	War Diary Of 8th. Bn. Lincolnshire Regiment for July 1916. 63/21		
Miscellaneous	A Form. Messages And Signals.		
War Diary	Ville	30/06/1916	30/06/1916
War Diary	Trenches Fricourt	01/07/1916	04/07/1916
War Diary	Dernancourt	04/07/1916	04/07/1916
War Diary	Vaux	05/07/1916	07/07/1916
War Diary	Talmas	08/07/1916	08/07/1916
War Diary	Mondicourt	10/07/1916	11/07/1916
War Diary	Hannescamps.	11/07/1916	14/07/1916
War Diary	Trenches	14/07/1916	14/07/1916
War Diary	Humber Camp	15/07/1916	15/07/1916
War Diary	Houvin	16/07/1916	17/07/1916
War Diary	Camblain	18/07/1916	18/07/1916
War Diary	L'Abbe.	19/07/1916	24/07/1916
War Diary	Trenches	25/07/1916	31/07/1916
Operation(al) Order(s)	Operation Orders No. 43 By Lieut Col. R.H. Johnston, D.S.O. Commanding 8th Battalion Lincolnshire Regiment. Sunday. 25th June, 1916	25/06/1916	25/06/1916
Miscellaneous	63rd Brigade Appendix X	05/07/1916	05/07/1916
Miscellaneous	Rom/ M.O. 8Lincoln Regt To./ A.D.M.S. 21st Division.	05/07/1917	05/07/1917

Woqs 2158/11

21ST DIVISION
63RD INFY BDE

8TH BN LINCOLNS. REGT
SEP 1915 - JLY 1916.

To 37 DIV 63 BDE

63rd Inf.Bde.
21st Div.

Battn. disembarked
Boulogne from
England 11.9.15.

8th BATTN. THE LINCOLNSHIRE REGIMENT.

S E P T E M B E R
(10.9.15-29.9.15)

1 9 1 5

Attached:

Appendix I.

WAR DIARY or INTELLIGENCE SUMMARY

Army Form C. 2118.

7TH (SERV) BN. LINCOLNSHIRE REGIMENT

Place	Date	Hour	Summary of Events and Information	Remarks and references to Appendices
WITLEY CAMP	10-9-15	7.10 P.M.	Bn. under the command of Lieut. Col. H.F. WALTER, left camp at 6 P.M. and entrained at MILFORD Stn. Journeyed via FOLKESTONE to BOULOGNE, in rest camp for 1 day; Officers 28 + 2 personnel 993 other ranks.	28.
BOULOGNE	11-9-15	7 P.M	Entrained at PONT des BRIQUES Stn for WATTEN; Billeted at BAYENGHEM-LES-EPERLECQUES.	28.
BAYENGHEM	17-9-15		Capt. Preston Harrison, Lieuts. Parker, Brown + Rowcroft spent 24 hrs. in the trenches of the 2nd. Corps. The first two Machine gun sections under Lieut. R.G. Gardiner were attached to 63rd Bde. Hdqrs. M.G. Detachment.	28.
	14.9.15		2nd Lt. Cragg and Sgt. Cummins + Wood attended a 4 days course of instruction at M.G. School at WISQUES. During stay at BAYENGHEM the Bn. participated in Brigade and Divisional Exercises and was also practised in bombing and in use of new pattern respirator.	28.
RACQUINGHEM	20-9-15	7 P.M.	Bn. left BAYENGHEM and bivouacked one night at RACQUINGHEM	28.
NORRENT	21-9-15	8.45 P.M.	Bn. left RACQUINGHEM and billeted at NORRENT.	28.
CAUCHY-a-TOUR	22-9-15	6.30 P.M	Bn left NORRENT and billeted at CAUCHY-a-TOUR. Bn addressed by Brig. Gen. N. NICKALLS Comdg. 63rd Inf. Bde.	28.
FOURS-a-CHAUX	24-9-15	1.30 P.M	Bn left CAUCHY-a-TOUR and bivouacked at FOURS-a-CHAUX 12mls from NOEUX-LES-MINES.	28.
	25-9-15	10.30 A.M.	Bn. with the 8th BN. SOMERSET L.I. was warned for the firing line.	28.
VERMELLES	25-9-15	2.30 P.M.	VERMELLES reached; under artillery fire:	28.
		7.10 P.M	Bn moved into position forming part of relieving force to the 15 Div. 24th Div. was on our left and the 8th BN. SOMERSET L.I. on our right.	28.

Army Form C. 2118

WAR DIARY or INTELLIGENCE SUMMARY

(Erase heading not required.)

8TH (SERV.) BN. LINCOLNSHIRE REGIMENT

Place	Date	Hour	Summary of Events and Information	Remarks and references to Appendices
VERMELLES	28-9-15	8.15 P.M.	Owing to casualties in Officers CAPT. H. PATTINSON became Act. Commander of the Bn.; Acting 2nd in Command CAPT. J.T. PRESTON; Acting Adjutant LIEUT. F. BROWN.	Acting 2B. 3A.
LINGHEM	29-9-15	9. A.M.	Bn. left VERMELLES and proceeded by road + rail to LINGHEM. Strength. 6 Officers + 2/personnel, O.R. 522.	

A P P E N D I X   I.

"A" Form.   Army Form C. 2121.
MESSAGES AND SIGNALS.

TO	A. General's Office
	G.H.Q.
	3rd Echelon Base.

Sender's Number.	Day of Month	In reply to Number		AAA
L3.	12	Second.		

Reference attached Appendix 1.
This information was supplied by
Acting C.S.M. J. W. Brown No.4. Coy.
" C.S.M. C. Lowe No.3 "
on the ground that all the officers, of
this unit who went into action on
the 25th – 27th, became casualties.

From Place: Shincoluker
Time: 1.40 pm

(Z) J. Brown Lt. A/Adjt.

APPENDIX I
Action near LOOS
25-27 SEPT. 1915.

VERMELLES.
25-9-15 6 P.M.

On the night of 25th Sept. our Bn. left the road leading to LOOS and formed lines of platoons in fours. After a short advance we halted for three hours. We then advanced in Echelon formation over the trenches. After advancing, for about three hours, in short stages, we halted for a short time and then moved in the direction of HILL 70.

We dug our ourselves in during the night. It was now daybreak.

Major Storer came to us and said "All is well." The advance will commence at 11 A.M. In the meantime we were under heavy shell and rifle fire. We then advanced meeting great numbers of the enemy. A short retirement took place the Bn. making a new line, of men composed of various unit, about 400x in rear of our first position.

We again advanced under the command of the nearest officer. By this time a great number of our officers had becomes casualties.

The men continued to fight with the units to which they had become attached.

On the 27th the Regiment was relieved by a unit of Guards.

Notes on 8th (S) Battn. Lincolnshire Regiment

by Captain F. Brown.

Adjt. 8/Lincoln.
63 Bde.
21 Div.
XV Corps

The 8th (S) Battn. Lincolnshire Regiment was formed in September 1914, a battalion of the 63rd Infantry Brigade and 21st Infantry Division.

Its first commanding officer was Lieut.-Colonel E.B. Wilkinson.

The brigade commander was Br.-General Fitz-Sody, and the divisional commander Lieut.-General Sir Edward T.H. Hutton KCB. KCMG.

Lieut.-Colonel E.B. Wilkinson was a Lincolnshire officer, having been adjutant and on the outbreak of war had been posted to the 6th (S) Battn. Lincolnshire Regiment as second-in-command. The newly-formed battalion concentrated in Halton Park near Tring and presented a most motley appearance, almost every form of dress was in evidence.

Gradually, however, clothing and boots were issued and more uniformity took the place of the somewhat harlequinade appearance.

The battalion moved into billets in Leighton Buzzard for the winter of 1914 and more arduous training began.

In the spring of 1915 the battalion moved to Halton Park Camp, Wendover, and miniature rifle practice began.

The chief officers of the battalion at this time were :-

```
Lieut.-Colonel E.B.Wilkinson......Commanding.
Major H.E.Walter..................second-in-command.
Capt. J.Topham....................Adjutant.
Capt. H.Coates....................O.C. "A" Company.
Capt. J.Storer....................O.C. "B" Company.
Capt. S.Stronguist................O.C. "C" Company.
Capt. L.McNaught Davis............O.C. "D" Company.
Lieut. F.Taylor...................Quartermaster.
Lieut. R.A.Ker....................Transport Officer.
```

With the completion of the firing of the Musketry Course and a Review of the division by Lord Kitchener, the battalion moved with the division by road to Witley Camp. This move occurred in August 1915 in sweltering heat and gave the battalion an indication of the strenuous days ahead.

En route to Witley Camp, Surrey, the battalion had the honour of marching past His Majesty The King and Lord Kitchener.

Final training was completed at Witley Camp and the battalion entrained for overseas at Milford Station near Witley 9th September 1915, under the command of Lieut.-Colonel H.E. Walters; Lieut.-Colonel E.B. Wilkinson having been appointed to the command of the 62nd Infantry Brigade. Travelling <u>via</u> Folkestone the battalion reached Boulogne 11th September 1915 and marched to the upper camp where a stay of a few days was made. A touch of reality was given to our stay at this place when iron rations were issued.

Then by rather strenuous stages chiefly by marching the battalion moved in the direction of Loos, although this destination was not generally known at the time.

While billeted at Les Epilecques, four officers of the battalion proceeded by motor omnibus to the line at Armentieres and spent 48 hours in the trenches. The use of gas in attack was being more extensively used, and our men were given instruction in the use of anti-gas measures en route for the line.

No casualties occurred en route and the division reached a position W. of Loos on 24th September 1915 and marched along the Mazingarbe - Philisophe road and deployed for action north of the road near Hulluch.

The battalion was severely engaged in the action which ensued and heavy casualties were sustained.

The officers named below were casualties in the action at Loos -

Lieut.-Colonel H.E.Walters..Commanding - Died of wounds at Douai.
Major Storer.................Second-in-command - Missing, since believed killed.
Captain Stronguist..........O.C."C" Coy - Killed in action.
Captain Coates..............O.C."A" Coy - Missing, since believed killed.
Captain E.M.Harrison........   Wounded.
Lieutenant E.N.Rowcroft.....   Wounded.
Captain J.Topham............Adjutant - Missing, since believed killed.
Captain L.McNaught Davis....O.C."D" Coy. - Wounded and taken prisoner.
Lieutenant F.H.G.Haldwell...O.C."B" Coy. - Wounded.

In fact all officers of the battalion actually going into action became casualties, and only four remained, these being ordered at the last moment to act as reserve, Capt.H.Pattinson being the senior surviving officer, assumed command and Capt.J.T.Preston became second-in-Command, and Capt. F.Brown, Adjutant. Capt H.Pattinson was eventually promoted Major and was one of the youngest Majors in the British Army, being barely 20 years of age. The task of reforming the battalion was a formidable one and Major R.H.G.Wilson, of the 1st Battalion, was appointed to command.

At the inspection of the battalion under the command of Major H.Pattinson by Major-General Forrestier Walker, the battalion was congratulated on its conduct during the recent operations at Loos.

After a period of rest for re-equipping and re-forming, the battalion moved to Armentieres and held the line from a point on the Armentieres - Lille road to L'Epinette, from October 1915 until March 1916.

Training of the battalion proceeded and gradually new N.C.O's were obtained which brought up the battalion to a more complete strength.

During the early part of November 1915 the battalion was unfortunate in losing its commanding officer (Lieut.-Colonel R.H.G.Wilson) who was wounded by a shell splinter while in the front trenches. This officer had directed the reforming of an almost fresh battalion as the majority of the officers and men in the original battalion had become casualties in the battalion's first action at Loos.

Major Taylor of the 10/York & Lancaster Regiment was appointed to the temporary command of the battalion.

Major Taylor reported his arrival at battalion headquarters in Armentieres and proceeding to his own billet for necessary kit was wounded en route by a fragment from a shell.

His tenure of command was a record for shortness being only about a quarter of an hour. Major Taylor was succeeded in the command of the battalion by Major R.H.Johnston DSO.

About this time - November 1915 - units from the 3rd Division replaced units in the 21st, and the 1/Lincolnshire joined the 62nd Infantry Brigade and the 4/Middlesex the 63rd Infantry Brigade.

It is interesting to note that the first commanding officer of the 4/Middlesex when it was formed was Lieut.-Colonel C.R.Simpson (now Major-General C.R.Simpson CB) the Colonel of the Lincolnshire Regiment.

When Major-General Simpson visited the battalions of the Lincolnshire Regiment in the field in 1917 he reviewed the 8th Battalion and the 4th Battn. Middlesex Regiment together on the same parade ground at Vielle Chapelle.

The winter of 1915 was very wet and the low lying stretches of trenches near Armentieres were generally under water.

Preventive measures to combat trench foot were necessary, and the battalion record for comparative immunity from this trouble was highly satisfactory.

This result was owing to the energetic efforts of the Medical Officer (Capt.H.Douglas Smart MD.RAMC) and the company officers under the direction of the commanding officer.

Drying rooms were erected in screened parts of the reserve line and systematic drying of the men's socks was carried out.

During the period of the tour in the Armentieres sector casualties were not excessive, and they chiefly occurred during the periods of stay in billets in the town of Armentieres. But during the last week of the battalion's stay in this sector the battalion lost four officers, three of whom were killed and one severely wounded.

The officers killed were :-

> Lieutenant G.E.L.Bowlby.
> Lieutenant R.B.Love.
> Lieutenant Fairweather.

The wounded officer was :-

> Lieutenant Phillips.

Towards the end of March 1916 the battalion moved as part of the 21st Division south to the line at Fricourt, rest billets being at Corbie.

During the period of training in rest billets area the battalion was trained including operations over trenches fac-similie to the German trenches opposite our lines in the Fricourt area.

The preliminary training for the Somme offensive was thorough, and those participating in the operation were well acquainted with the German trenches as a result of the practice carried out at the divisional training area at Corbie.

All the company commanders taking part in the operations on the 1st July 1916 were casualties.

Capts. E.R.Devonshire, R.G.Cordiner, G.C.Lafferty, commanding "A","C" and "D" Companies respectively, were wounded and Captain A.C.Jones, commanding "B" Coy. was killed in action

Capt.R.G.Cordiner and Lieut.R.A.Preston were awarded the Military Cross for gallantry during these operations.

Owing to heavy casualties suffered by the 63rd Infantry Brigade it was transferred to the 37th Division and moved for a period of rest to Hannescamp and the 8/Lincolnshire held the line there relieving the 2/5th (T.F.) Lincolnshire.

This tour of duty was the quietest the battalion experienced.

After a short stay at Hannescamp the battalion moved by road to take part in the operations at Beaumont Hamel. Following on the heels of the Naval Division the battalion made a useful find. A mess cart with a cracked axle was discovered discarded by the affluent Naval Division, and by a blacksmith's manoeuvre was taken on unofficial charge as an additional mess cart.

The very wet conditions which prevailed during the Ancre operations caused many casualties through sickness. The difficulty of heating food in the forward areas was overcome by the issue of solidified alcohol which gave off heat without causing smoke, being a great advantage.

After four days of attack and consolidation the battalion was withdrawn to the reserve line, but was moved forward after two days in reserve to relieve the 6/Bradford who had suffered severe casualties.

Eventually in the first week in December the

battalion was withdrawn and moved to Mesnil and from thence to Sarton where it was re-equipped and reformed.

In December 1916 Lieut.-Colonel R.H.Johnston DSO. relinquished command after being in command continuously since November 1915.

Lieut.-Colonel E.A.Cameron succeeded him. During the stay in Sarton the battalion was reviewed by the corps commander, Lieut.-General Fanshawe, who congratulated the battalion on its appearance and turn out.

The battalion then moved into the line at Neuve Chapelle and was billeted at Leistrem spending the Christmas of 1916 there. Early in January 1917 Lieut.-Colonel Cameron was wounded and Major H.Pattinson assumed temporary command till the arrival of Major D.W.C.Davis-Evans (Pembroke Yeomanry) who then took up command.

At the end of February the battalion returned to the scene of its first action - Loos - and was billeted at Maringarbe.

The trenches at Loos had been built under great difficulties during the period of consolidation in 1915 after the action at Loos and revetting had not generally been done.

As the frost gave way towards the end of February 1917, the conditions of the trenches was bad, and much work had to be done to make them passable; all available divisional troops being put on this task and by almost superhuman effort the trenches were made passable and fit to be handed over to relieving forces.

The first week in March 1917 the battalion moved from Loos to take part in the attack on the Arras front planned for 9th April 1917.

The battalion moved through Arras on Easter Monday and when crossing the bridge about 200 to 300 yards south of the station the commanding officer and adjutant were narrowly missed by a small shell which skimmed the bridge and fell to the railway below igniting a small dump of petrol which for some reason or other had been placed near a battery under the bridge.

This shell eventually caused the destruction of the bridge and battalions in the rear of the column, 4/Middlesex and 10/York and Lancaster, suffered casualties from the debris made where the shells exploded. The report of this explosion was terrific.

The battalion moving forward through the cemetery at Arras rested for a short time near Orange Hill.

Much of the enemy wire which was thickly placed had not been cut by the guns but fairly good progress was maintained by crossing the wire zones along the tracks left by the tanks.

Eventually the battalion reached Lone Copse, a sheltered valley and here it reformed. Violent bursts of shrapnel from the enemy were experienced and it was obvious the enemy had the range of this sheltered place from which he had so recently been ousted.

At a point in this action ammunition was very low and the attack, on Monchy le Preux, which was impending had not been embarked on. It was necessary to get ammunition and that quickly.

All telephone communications had been cut and the constant shelling of the valley near Line Copse repeatedly severed wires which the signals had tried to repair.

Fortunately a pigeon remained but the disc for fitting on the leg of the pigeon was gone.

The adjutant, however, wrote a message requesting ammunition and water to be sent up to the line, tore out a thread of wool from a stocking and fastening the message to the bird released the bird wishing it luck on its journey. The bird reached the divisional cage and the ammunition was brought up in the evening. This eased a somewhat critical position.

In the attack on Monchy le Preux Lieut.-Colonel F.W. Greatwood was severely wounded in the arm which eventually necessitated amputation.

Lieut.-Colonel Greatwood's cool, fearless and able leading during the attack inspired all ranks. For his conduct in this operation he was awarded the D.S.O.

The battalion was withdrawn for rest and refitting on or about 28th April 1917, and moved into Arras and from thence to its billeting area.

During the operations around Arras the battalion had received no reinforcements and its strength had become greatly depleted.

After two days partial rest during which company rolls were checked and the men re-equipped, training was recommenced.

(sgd) F. BROWN.

21/53

12/7595

21st Kirwin

8th December
Part of vol I

Nov 15

Army Form C. 2118

WAR DIARY
or
INTELLIGENCE SUMMARY
(Erase heading not required.)

Instructions regarding War Diaries and Intelligence Summaries are contained in F.S. Regs., Part II. and the Staff Manual respectively. Title Pages will be prepared in manuscript.

ORDERLY ROOM
No. ....
Date 31.10.15
1ST (SERVY.) BN. LINCOLNSHIRE REGIMENT

Place	Date	Hour	Summary of Events and Information	Remarks and references to Appendices
LINGHEM	1-10-15	7.30 AM	Bn. left LINGHEM and billeted at STEENBECQUE	7B
STEENBECQUE	2.10.15	8.30 AM	Bn. left STEENBECQUE and marched to BORRÉ and billeted; 2½ mls. N.E. HAZEBROUCK.	8B
BORRÉ	6.10.15	6 P.M.	Bn. received reinforcement 4 officers and 40 men from the 3rd Bn. 2nd Lt. LATHAM; R.A. PRESTON; E.A. DAFF; L.J.E.C. FAIRWEATHER.	8B
	7.10.15	10 AM	Brig. Gen. E.R. HILL H.L.I. reviewed officers and men of new draft.	8B
	8.10.15	2.30 PM	Major Gen. G.T. FORESTIER-WALKER C.B. Commanding 21st Div. reviewed the Bn. and afterwards addressed the officers.	9B
	9.10.15	6.15 P.M.	Reinforcement of 8 officers. 2nd Lt. L.D. EDWARDS, T.S. BOADLE, G.E.L. BOWLEY, W.H. STEPHENS, N.S. DOUGALL, S. FERRY, W.J. TYSON, S. PHILLIPPS.	7B
	10-10-15		MAJOR R. H.G. WILSON of the 2nd LINCOLNSHIRE REGT. having been posted to this Bn. arrived and assumed command of the Bn. from this date. CAPT. H. PATTINSON having vacated acting command of the Bn. assumed the duties of 2nd in Command from this date.	11 / 11
	11.10.15	6 P.M.	1 Officer 2nd Lt. V. SMITH and 58 men arrived.	
	13.10.15		Reinforcement of 6 officers. 2nd Lt. C.D. JESSOPP, A. LILL, E.B. MARKHAM, E.R. DEVONSHIRE, R. B. LOVE, F.L. GOOSEMAN.	8B
STRAZEELE	15-10-15	2 P.M.	Bn. left BORRÉ for STRAZEELE	
	19.10.15	8 AM	Bn. with YORK + LANCASTER inspected by the Corps General Sir HENRY FERGUSON C.B. who addressed the Bn. on trench warfare.	8B
	23.10.15	4 P.M	Lt. CORDINER sustained injury to foot whilst undergoing instruction in bombing.	8B

WAR DIARY or INTELLIGENCE SUMMARY

Army Form C. 2118

Place	Date	Hour	Summary of Events and Information	Remarks and references to Appendices
STRAZEELE	24.10.15	9 A.M.	Bn. left STRAZEELE for la BECQUE.	
ARMENTIERES	26.10.15	1.30 P.M	Bn. left la BECQUE area for billets in ARMENTIERES. Transport parked in field 2½ mls. from Bn. Hdqr. Remainder of month Bn. occupied in supplying men for C.R.E 50th Div. at work on TRENCH DEFENCES.	
	31.10.15	10.30 P.M	Reinforcement of 79 N.C.Os and men arrived from 3rd Bn. Fighting strength. Officers 23 O.R. 603.	App. 1. Officers 31-10-15

Appendix 2 officers.

8TH (SERV) BN. LINCOLNSHIRE REGIMENT

Roll of Officers by Companies.

Rank & Name	Date of gazette	Date of joining	Qualifications	Remarks
Major. R. H. G. Wilson.		10. 10. 15.		Commanding Officer
Captain. H. Pattinson.				Act. Second in Command
Lieut. F. Brown.				Act Adjutant
Lt. & Qr. Mr. F. Taylor.				
No. 1. Company				
Captain. J. S. Preston.				
Lieut. R. A. Het.			Transport.	
2nd Lieut. C. D. Jessopp.		13. 10. 15.		
" S. Ferry.		9. 10. 15.		
" F. G. Tyson.		9. 10. 15.		
" V. Smith.		11. 10. 15.	Signalling.	
" E. M. Carre.		1. 11. 15.		
(Interpreter Belgian) *				* For Rations.
No. 2. Company.				
2nd Lieut. E. A. Duff.		6. 10. 15.		
" S. Phillips.		9. 10. 15.		
" L. D. Edwards.		9. 10. 15.		
" L. F. E. C. Fairweather.		6. 10. 15.	Machine Gun	
" A. Gill.		13. 10. 15.		
" E. B. Markham.		13. 10. 15.		
" C. H. Rhodes.	posted but not yet joined			
No. 3. Company.				
2nd Lieut. L. A. Preston.		6. 10. 15.		
" J. W. Latham.		6. 10. 15.		
" N. S. Dougall.		9. 10. 15.	Bombing.	
" E. R. Devonshire.		13. 10. 15.		
" R. B. Love.		13. 10. 15.		
" D. C. Hodgson.	posted but not joined this unit.			
No. 4. Company.				
Lieut. R. G. Cordeux.				
2nd Lieut. G. E. L. Bowlby.		9. 10. 15.	Range taking	
" W. H. Stephens.		9. 10. 15.		
" J. S. Boadle.		9. 10. 15.		
" F. L. Gooseman.		13. 10. 15.		
" A. C. Jones.		1. 11. 15.		
(Interpreter French) *				* For Rations.

F. Brown Lt & Act.
ADJUTANT
8TH (SERV) BN. LINCOLNSHIRE REGIMENT.

ORDERLY ROOM
Date 31-10-15
8TH (SERV) BN. LINCOLNSHIRE REGIMENT

21st Novr

$\frac{121}{7631}$

J. A. Lawton
Lot 2

Nov. 15

WAR DIARY or INTELLIGENCE SUMMARY

Army Form C. 2118

8 Lincolnshire Regiment

Place	Date	Hour	Summary of Events and Information	Remarks and references to Appendices
ARMENTIERES	1/11/15		Bn. in billets. Town shelled, 2nd Lts. H.C. JONES and E.M. CARRE arrived.	N⁰ to O.O.
ARMENTIERES	2/11/15		Bn. in billets.	N⁰ to O.O.
"	3/11/15	4 pm / 5:30 pm	½ Bn. entered trenches 81-89 for instruction under 6th DLI, 9th DLI and 5th Loyal N. Lancs. reg. D. 2nd Lt. C. RHODES arrived.	N⁰ to O.O.
"	4/11/15		½ Bn. in trenches.	N⁰ to O.O.
"	5/11/15	4:30 pm / 5:30 pm	2nd half Bn. relieved 1st half for similar instruction (48 hrs). Rifles firing at 6:30 pm.	N⁰ to O.O.
"	6/11/15		½ Bn. in trenches, 2 wounded.	N⁰ to O.O.
"	7/11/15	4:30 pm / 5:30 pm	2nd half Bn. returned to billets.	N⁰ to O.O.
"	8/11/15	4:30 pm / 5:30 pm	Bn. entered trenches 81-89 for 48 hrs instruction under 7th DLI, 9th DLI & 5th Loyal N. Lancs. reg.	N⁰ to O.O.
"	9/11/15		Bn. in trenches.	N⁰ to O.O.
"	10/11/15	5 pm / 6 pm	Bn. left the trenches.	N⁰ to O.O.
"	11/11/15	3 pm	Bn. moved to new billets near station. Period of instruction ended.	N⁰ to O.O.
"	12/11/15		Bn. in billets.	N⁰ to O.O.
"	13/11/15	5:05 pm / 6:05 pm	Bn. took over from 12th W. York Regt. trenches 67-69 as follows:- n⁰ 4 co. 67 T. n⁰ 2 co. 68 T. n⁰ 1 co. 69 T. n⁰ 3 co. LILLE POST garrison. *	N⁰ to O.O. * App 2.
"	14/11/15		Bn. in trenches, Germans reported relieved in evening.	N⁰ to O.O.
"	15/11/15		Bn. in trenches, 1 killed 1 wounded.	N⁰ to O.O.
"	16/11/15		Bn. in trenches.	N⁰ to O.O.

WAR DIARY or INTELLIGENCE SUMMARY

Army Form C. 2118

Place	Date	Hour	Summary of Events and Information	Remarks and references to Appendices
ARMENTIERES	17/11/15		Bⁿ in trenches. Our artillery active in morning. Lieut. Bd. R.H.G. WILSON and 2nd Lieut N.S. DOUGALL wounded. 1 man killed 1 wounded. Bⁿ relieved by 4th Middlesex Reg^t returned to old billets.	W.D. (a9).
"	18/11/15	12 non 11 p.m.	Vicinity of billets shelled. Major TAYLOR 10th Y&L Reg^t assumed Comm^d 2nd Lt. Major TAYLOR & 6 men wounded. Major R.H. JOHNSTON 2nd Lincolnshire Reg^t assumed command of the Bⁿ.	W.D. (b) P.M.P.S.
"	19/11/15		Bⁿ in billets.	W.D. (c) 4.M.
"	20/11/15		Bⁿ in billets.	W.D. (d) P.M.
"	21/11/15	5.0 P.M 6 p.m.	Bⁿ relieved 4th Middlesex in trenches 67 to 60. Dispositions as before.	W.D. P.M.
"	22/11/15		Bⁿ in trenches.	W.D. P.M.
"	23/11/15		Bⁿ in trenches. 2nd Lieut B.G.L. BEARD & 9 NCOs & men arrived. 1 man killed 2 wounded.	W.D. P.M.
"	24/11/15		Bⁿ in trenches. Our artillery active to left. 2nd Lieut F.L. GOOSEMAN & 1 man wounded. 2nd Lt. GOOSEMAN returned to duty	W.D. P.M.
"	25/11/15		69 Trench shelled. In G. emplacement hit. 3 killed. 6 wounded. Bⁿ relieved by 4th Middlesex. Capt. J.T. PRESTON sent to hospital.	W.D. P.M.
"	26/11/15		Bⁿ in billets.	W.D. P.M.
"	27/11/15		Bⁿ in billets. Town shelled in vicinity of square.	W.D. P.M.

Army Form C. 2118

WAR DIARY
or
INTELLIGENCE SUMMARY

(Erase heading not required.)

Instructions regarding War Diaries and Intelligence Summaries are contained in F. S. Regs., Part II. and the Staff Manual respectively. Title Pages will be prepared in manuscript.

Place	Date	Hour	Summary of Events and Information	Remarks and references to Appendices
ARMENTIÈRES	28/11/15		Bn. in billets.	McA/P
"	29/11/15		Bn. relieved 4th Middlesex in trenches 67-69 as follows. 67 T. No 2 co. 68 T. No 3 co. 69 T. No 4 co. LILLE POST garrison No 1 co. Gun artillery active in vicinity.	McA/P RA1
"	30/11/15		Bn. in trenches. British airmen brought down into German lines by rifle fire. Aircraft track 66.	McA/P RA1
			Total Strength Officers 30. Other Ranks 709 Fighting Strength Officers other Ranks 564 both Br. O = 21 Details 9	

R/H Johnston. Major
Comdg 8th Lincolnshire

1875 Wt. W593/826 1,000,000 4/15 J.B.C. & A. A.D.S.S./Forms/C. 2118.

SECRET.

Appendix 2. Map of Trenches 67 to 69.

69   68   67

PIGOT'S FARM

GUARDS FARM

CLOSE SUPPORTS 67.

LOTHIAN AVENUE

SPIGOT LINE SUPPORTS

LEITH WALK

HAYSTACK FARM

DUMP & LIGHTS

TRENCH LILLE POST

LILLE POST Bn H.Q.

CEMETERY.

SQUARE FARM Bn. BATTLE H.Q.

DUMP

SCALE 1 : 2556 YARDS.
1 inch = 71 y'ds

FIELD DRESSING STATION

Appendix III.

Roll of Officers by Companies.

Rank & Name	Date of Gazette	Date of joining	Qualifications	
Major R. H. G. Wilson	—	10-10-15	C.O.	wounded 16/11/15
Major R. H. Johnston D.S.O.	—	17-11-15	C.O.	
Capt. H. Pattenson	19-9-14	19-9-14	2nd in C.	
Lieut. F. Brown	19-12-14	19-12-14	Adjutant	
Lt. & Q.M. F. Taylor	10-3-15	10-3-15		

No. 1 Company.

Capt. J. T. Preston	19-9-14	19-9-14	O.C. no.1 co.	to hospital 25/11/15
Lieut. R. A. Ker	22-9-14	22-9-14	Transport	
2nd Lt. C. D. Jessopp	22-9-14	13-10-15		
" S. Ferry	4-1-15	9-10-15	bombing	
" W. J. Tyson	7-1-15	9-10-15		
" V. E. A. Smith	22-12-14	11-10-15	signalling	
" E. M. Carré	3-10-15	1-11-15	(at Grenade School)	

(L. Habot. Belgian interpreter).

No. 2 Company

2nd Lieut. A. C. Jones	3-10-15	1-11-15	O.C. no.2 co.	
" J. Phillips	24-12-14	9-10-15	No.2 co. bombing officer	
" L. D. Edwards	16-9-14	9-10-15		
" Lg. E. C. Fairweather	21-5-15	6-10-15	M.G.	
" A. Lill	25-2-15	13-10-15	(68th Fd. Ambulance)	
" E. B. Markham	27-3-15	13-10-15		
" C. W. Rhodes	3-10-15	3-11-15	Intelligence training	

No. 3 Company.

2nd Lieut. R. A. Preston	24-4-15	6-10-15	O.C. no.3 co.	
" T. W. Latham	24-4-15	6-10-15	No.3 co. bombing officer	
" E. A. Duff	2-5-15	6-10-15		
" N. S. Dougall	25-1-15	9-10-15	bombing	(wounded 16/11/15)
" E. R. Devonshire	26-1-15	13-10-15	O.C. no.1 co.	
" R. B. Love	27-3-15	13-10-15		
" D. C. Hodgson	3-10-15	—		sick, not yet joined

No. 4 Company.

Lieut. R. G. Cordiner	20-9-14	20-9-14		accidentally wounded 23-10-15 rejoined 1/12/15

Rank & Name	Date of gazette	Date of joining	qualifications	Remarks
2nd Lt. G. E. L. Bowlby.	9-12-14	9-10-15	Range taking	
" W. H. Stephens.	21-1-15	9-10-15	Mining	
" T. S. Boadle.	2-11-14	9-10-15	No 4 co. bombing officer.	
" F. L. Grossman.	11-3-15	13-10-15	(at Class of Instruction Trench Warfare)	
" R. G. L. Beard.	—	23-11-15	Reserve M.G.	

1/12/15

R. H. Johnston Major
Cmdg. 8th Line R.

File The Arabs
Vol: 3
December 1915

WAR DIARY or INTELLIGENCE SUMMARY

Army Form C. 2118

(Erase heading not required.)

Place	Date	Hour	Summary of Events and Information	Remarks and references to Appendices
ARMENTIÈRES	1/12/15		Bn in Trenches. Lieut R. G. CORDINER rejoined Bn in Trenches. Front quiet. 2 men slightly wounded (whizzbang).	N/5 off. RW7
"	2/12/15		Bn in trenches. CHAPELLE D'ARMENTIÈRES shelled in morning & night (mostly shrapnel). 1 man wounded (sniper).	N/5 off. RW7
"	3/12/15	5.0 pm to 8-0 pm	Bn relieved by 4th Middlesex & returned to billets. Front quiet.	N/5 off. RW7
"	4/12/15		Bn in billets. Vicinity of billets shelled 4:30 pm to 6:0 pm. about 12 H.E. shells of about 6 to 8 inch. No billets injured beyond glass & windows broken.	N/5 off. RW7
"	5/12/15		Bn in billets. Few shells in town about 3-45 pm.	N/5 off. R.O.T.
"	6/12/15.		Bn in billets.	N/5 off. R.O.T.
"	7/12/15	6-0 pm to 8-0 pm	Bn relieved 4th Middlesex in Trenches 67 to 69. Dispositions as on 29/11/15.	N/5 off. R.O.T.
"	8/12/15.		Bn in trenches, 12 mm to 11 am. 6 in artillery bombarded front line trenches & 2 machine guns fired from LILLE POST on WEZ MACQUART. 67 Trench shelled with H.E. (about 4:2 & about 6 in mortars). 3 killed (H.E.) 1 slightly wounded (=duty).	N/5 off. RW7
"	9-12-15		Bn in trenches. Front line trenches shelled. No 2 m.g. emplacement damaged by H.E. ARMENTIÈRE RES. shelled by about 400 shells (H.E. 6 & 8 inch). H.Q. billet slightly damaged, 1 killed (H.E.) 5 wounded (1 to duty. 1 died of wounds 10/12/15).	N/5 off. RW7
"	10/12/15	about 10-30 p.m.	Bn in trenches. Germans heard shouting. Relief believed to have been effected by Saxons. 1 man wounded.	N/5 off. RW7
"	11/12/15		Bn in trenches. Intermittent artillery firing throughout day on flanks. 1 man wounded.	N/5 off. RW7

WAR DIARY or INTELLIGENCE SUMMARY

Army Form C. 2118

Instructions regarding War Diaries and Intelligence Summaries are contained in F. S. Regs., Part II. and the Staff Manual respectively. Title Pages will be prepared in manuscript.

(Erase heading not required.)

Place	Date	Hour	Summary of Events and Information	Remarks and references to Appendices
ARMENTIÈRES	12/12/15		Bⁿ in Trenches. Both sides very quiet indeed. 70 men reinforcements from Base	
"	13/12/15	5pm to 8pm	Bⁿ relieved by 4 R. Middlesex & returned to old billets.	
"	14/12/15		Bⁿ in billets. 3 Lieuts & Colonels attached Bⁿ for 3 days instruction.	
"	15/12/15		Bⁿ in billets.	
"	16/12/15		Bⁿ in billets. 3-15am 2 Platoons Somerset L.I. entered German trench opposite trench 70 & took several prisoners.	
"	17/12/15		Bⁿ in billets. Further to note of 16/12/15 at German machine gun was captured but lost 6-0	
"			4ft in depth - estimated German casualties 50	
"	18/12/15		Bⁿ in billets	
"	19/12/15		Bⁿ relieved 4 R. Middlesex in trenches 67, 6, 69. Dispositions - (67 No 1 Coy. 68 No 2 Coy 69 No 3 Coy 4 Coy)	
			Enemy exploded two mines opposite Mountrevan (trench 70) (Lille Post No 4 Coy)	
"			Our artillery opened heavy fire - enemy replying in trenches 67 & 70. No casualties	
"	20/12/15		Bⁿ in trenches - both sides quiet. Casualties - 2nd Lt Smith (Chandler) and 1 man, both wounded	
"	21/12/15		Bⁿ in trenches - conditions normal. 70 men reinforcements from Base	
"	22/12/15		Bⁿ in trenches - Our artillery bombarded enemy lines from 11-10 am to 3-30 pm with good result. Enemy replying on our front but without result	

Army Form C. 2118

WAR DIARY
or
INTELLIGENCE SUMMARY
(Erase heading not required.)

Instructions regarding War Diaries and Intelligence Summaries are contained in F. S. Regs., Part II. and the Staff Manual respectively. Title Pages will be prepared in manuscript.

Place	Date	Hour	Summary of Events and Information	Remarks and references to Appendices
ARMENTIERES	23/12/15		B" in Trenches, relieved by 4th Middlesex at 7-30 p.m. and returned to billets	Appdx (A?)
"	24/12/15		B" in billets	Appdx AM
"	25/12/15		B" in billets	Appdx RM
"	26/12/15		B" in billets. C.O. away on base line	Appdx RM
"	27/12/15		B" relieved 4th Middlesex in Trenches — dispositions as previously. C.O. returned from line	Appdx RM
"	28/12/15		B" in Trenches — ordinary quiet	Appdx RM
"	29/12/15		B" in Trenches (2 casualties — no deal of wounds)	Appdx RM
"	30/12/15		B" in Trenches (3 casualties — no deal of wounds) 2nd Lt Rayfield (from 2nd Lo'rd heavy Regt) joined the Battalion	Appdx RM
"	31/12/15		B" in Trenches, relieved by 4th Middlesex at 7-20 p.m. and returned to billets	Appdx RM.

R.H. Johnston
Major
Comdg.

List of Casualties during month of Sep 1915

	Through Sickness		Wounded	Killed	Remarks
	Reports Sick	F.A. Hospital			
In trenches	21	8	12×	4	× wounded & slightly wounded at duty
In billets	150	29	1	Nil	
Total	201	37	13	4	
Rejoined	7	1	1	—	
	30		12	—	

Officers: 2/Lt L.E.A. Smith wounded in trenches 20/9/15
31 12/15

Rlt. Johnston Major
Comdg

10TH (SERV) BN. LINCOLNSHIRE REGIMENT.

Copy

List of Reinforcements arrived during the month of December 1915

Date	Officers Rank & Name	Other Ranks	Remarks
12/12/15	Nil	70	
21/12/15	Nil	70	
30/12/15	1	—	
Total	1	140	

R.H. Johnston Major
Commdg

31/12/15

St. Lucolm.

rot: 4.
Tan 16

WAR DIARY or INTELLIGENCE SUMMARY

Army Form C. 2118

(Erase heading not required.)

Instructions regarding War Diaries and Intelligence Summaries are contained in F.S. Regs., Part II. and the Staff Manual respectively. Title Pages will be prepared in manuscript.

Place	Date	Hour	Summary of Events and Information	Remarks and references to Appendices
ARMENTIERES	1-1-16		Bn in Billets. A. Number 23/15. Bn commenced leave under Brigade arrangements (percentage pantie of 10)	Appx RM7
"	2-1-16		Bn in Billets	Appx RM7
"	3-1-16		Bn in Billets	Appx RM7
"	4-1-16		Bn relieved 4th MIDDLESEX in trenches. Dispositions - Trench 69 No 3 - Trench 68 No 1 - Trench 69 No 4 - LILLE POST No 1. 1 casualty.	Appx RM7
"	5-1-16		Bn in Trenches. Normal.	Appx RM7
"	6-1-16		Bn in Trenches. Trench 69 heavily bombarded. Casualties 1 killed, 9 wounded (one severe)	Appx RM7 RM7
"	7-1-16		Bn in Trenches. Normal	Appx RM7
"	8-1-16		Bn in Trenches. Our artillery bombarded enemy front line who retaliated on Trenches 68 and 69. Casualties 4 wounded (all slight) Bn relieved by 4th MIDDLESEX at 7-30 pm and returned to billets.	Appx RM7
"	9-1-16		Bn in Billets	Appx RM7
"	10-1-16		Bn in Billets	Appx RM7
"	11-1-16		Bn in Billets	Appx RM7 RM7 Appx
"	12-1-16		Bn in Billets - relieved 8TH SOMERSETS in trenches. Dispositions - Trench 70. H.Q. and entrenching tools. Nos 1 and 2 - Trench 71 and 72a. No 3 - Trench 72b and 73. No 4. Condition of trenches very bad especially in Trench 70 and MUSHROOM - sides in a mud very soft. Sides flatten to enable parties to pass. and finding parts consisted only of small sandbag barrier.	RM7 Appx

Army Form C. 2118

Instructions regarding War Diaries and Intelligence Summaries are contained in F. S. Regs, Part II. and the Staff Manual respectively. Title Pages will be prepared in manuscript.

WAR DIARY
or
INTELLIGENCE SUMMARY
(Erase heading not required.)

Place	Date 1916	Hour	Summary of Events and Information	Remarks and references to Appendices
ARMENTIERES	13-1-16		B⁰⁰ in Trenches - 2 casualties (slight - 1 returned to duty)	RM/1/16
	14-1-16		B⁰⁰ in Trenches - Trench 71 and 72a heavily shelled - no casualties or damage, shells mostly landing just behind trench. 6 inch about 29. 7.7cm about 20	
	15-1-16		B⁰⁰ relieved in Trenches by 4TH MIDDLESEX at 8-15 p.m. 1 casualty (slight)	RM/1/16
	16-1-16		B⁰⁰ in Billets (ARMENTIÈRES (vicinity Brewers' H.Q.) shelled about 7.30 p.m. 7.7cm about 20	Appd RM/1
	17-1-16		B⁰⁰ in Billets - see note above	Appd RM/1
	18-1-16		B⁰⁰ in Billets	Appd RM/1
	19-1-16		B⁰⁰ in Billets	Appd RM/1
	19-1-16		B⁰⁰ relieved 4TH MIDDLESEX in Trenches (1 casualty - wounded) Dispositions - Trench 70 and adjoining lines No 3 in Trench 71. 72A-No 1. Trench 72-73-No 2	Appd RM/1
	20-1-16		B⁰⁰ in Trenches - 2 casualties (1 killed, 1 wounded)	Appd RM/1
	21-1-16		B⁰⁰ in Trenches - 1 casualty (killed)	Appd RM/1
	22-1-16		B⁰⁰ in Trenches - 2 casualties (2 wounded)	Appd RM/1
	23-1-16		B⁰⁰ relieved in Trenches by 4TH MIDDLESEX at 7.50 p.m. 2 casualties (wounded)	Appd RM/1
	24-1-16		B⁰⁰ in Billets	Appd RM/1
	25-1-16		B⁰⁰ in Billets. Road of 6 adjoining huts hit 7 p.m. during attack by DIVISIONAL CYCLISTS, returning to billets at 1-45 p.m.	Appd RM/1
	26-1-16		B⁰⁰ in Billets	Appd RM/1
	27-1-16		B⁰⁰ relieved 4TH MIDDLESEX in Trenches. Dispositions - Nos 1 and 2 - Trench 70 to adjoining line No 3 Trench 72(B) and 73 No 4 Trench 71 and 72(a).	Appd RM/1

WAR DIARY / INTELLIGENCE SUMMARY

Army Form C. 2118

Place	Date 1916	Hour	Summary of Events and Information	Remarks and references to Appendices
ARMENTIÈRES	28-1-16		B² in Trenches. H.Q. at FIVE DUG OUTS heavily bombarded from 2-15 p.m. to 4-15 p.m.	Appdx RM7
			Trench 70 heavily shelled. 2 casualties (slight)	
	29-1-16		B² in Trenches. H.Q. moved down to front immediately behind where SUBSIDIARY LINES	Appdx RM7
			meet PORTE EGAL AVENUE. 5 DUG OUTS again shelled	
	30-1-16		B² in Trenches. 3 casualties (1 killed)	Appdx RM7
	31-1-16		B² in Trenches. 3 casualties (1 killed, 1 officer returned to duty)	Appdx RM7

2 BROWN Col T Alf Jr. LT. COLONEL,
COMDG. 8TH (SERV.) BN. LINCOLNSHIRE REGIMENT

ROLL OF OFFICERS — 8TH BN LINCOLNSHIRE REGT

Rank	Name	Date of Gazette	Date of Joining	Remarks
Lieut Col.	R. H. Johnston, D.S.O.		18-11-15	Commanding
Capt	H. Pattinson	19. 9. 14.	19. 9. 14.	Actg 2nd in command
"	F. Brown	19. 12. 14.	19. 12. 14.	Actg Adjutant
Lt. & Qr. Mr.	F. Taylor	10. 3. 15.	10. 3. 15.	
Lieut	R. A. Ker	22. 9. 14.	25. 9. 14.	Transport
2nd Lieut	L. J. E. C. Fairweather	21. 5. 15.	6. 10. 15.	Machine Gun Officer
"	B. J. L. Beard	11. 2. 15.	13. 10. 15.	Intelligence & Sniping Officer
"	S. Terry	4. 1. 15.	9. 10. 15.	Bn Grenadier Officer
NO 1 COMPANY				
2nd Lieut	E. R. Devonshire	26. 1. 15.	13. 10. 15.	O.C. Company
"	C. W. Rhodes	3. 10. 15.	3. 11. 15.	P. Comdr. Grenade course
"	W. J. Tyson	7. 1. 15.	9. 10. 15.	P. Comdr.
"	E. M. Carre	3. 10. 15.	1. 11. 15.	P. Comdr. Coy Grenadier Officer
"	F. W. Latham	24. 4. 15.	6. 10. 15.	P. Comdr.
NO 2 COMPANY				
Lieut	A. C. Jones	3. 10. 15.	1. 11. 15.	O.C. Company
2nd Lieut	L. D. Edwards	16. 9. 14.	9. 10. 15.	P. Comdr.
"	S. Phillips	24. 12. 14.	9. 10. 15.	P. Comdr. Coy Grenadier Officer
"	A. Fill	25. 2. 15.	13. 10. 15.	P. Comdr.
"	E. B. Markham	27. 3. 15.	13. 10. 15.	P. Comdr. Grenadier Officer
NO 3 COMPANY				
Lieut	R. G. Gardiner	20. 9. 14.		O.C. Coy. Training in M.G. R.F.
2nd Lt	C. D. Jessopp	22. 9. 14.	13. 10. 15.	P. Comdr. Coy Grenadier Officer
"	R. A. Preston	24. 4. 15.	6. 10. 15.	Course at TERGHEM. P. Comdr.
"	R. B. Love	27. 3. 15.	13. 10. 15.	P. Comdr.
"	E. A. Duff	2. 5. 15.	6. 10. 15.	P. Comdr.
NO 4 COMPANY				
2nd Lieut	G. E. L. Bowlby	9. 12. 14.	9. 10. 15.	O.C. Company
"	J. S. Boadle	2. 11. 14.	9. 10. 15.	Coy Grenadier Officer. P. Comdr.
"	W. H. Stephens	21. 1. 15.	9. 10. 15.	Att 182 Tunnelling Coy.
"	F. L. Gorseman	11. 3. 15.	13. 10. 15.	P. Comdr.
"	J. Kendall	10. 1. 16.	30. 12. 15.	Sick whilst on leave
"	R. L. Courtice	16. 1. 16.	21. 1. 16.	P. Comdr.
"	W. J. Haward	16. 1. 16.	21. 1. 16.	P. Comdr.

Copy

Casualties incurred during the month of January 1916

	Through Sickness	Wounded	Killed	Remarks
In Trenches	1 x	x 19	37	
In Billets	19 x	1	Nil	

x These are the Casualties evacuated

R.J. Winter Lieut Col
Comdg 8th (Serv) Bn. LINCOLNSHIRE REGIMENT

6"V"

St Thomas's
Feb 1916

Army Form C. 2118

WAR DIARY
or
INTELLIGENCE SUMMARY
(Erase heading not required.)

Place	Date	Hour	Summary of Events and Information	Remarks and references to Appendices
ARMENTIÈRES	1-2-16		Bn. returned to trenches by 9th SOMERSETS and returned to billets. 1 casualty (wounded)	Appdx A1
	2-2-16		Bn. in billets	App. A117
	3-2-16		Bn. in billets	App. A117
	4-2-16		Bn. relieved 10 YORK & LANCAST ER REGT. and moved into trenches night 4/5. right sector.	App. A117
	5-2-16		Bn. in trenches (no casualties)	App. A117
	6-2-16		Bn. in trenches (no casualties)	App. A117
	7-2-16		Bn. in trenches (1 casualty R.E. working party.)	App. A117
			Bn. relieved in trenches by 12. Bn. NORTHUMBERLAND FUSILIERS.	App. A117
			Bn. returned to billet in new area of the town.	App. A117
	8-2-16		Bn. received draft of 49 men (including 7 men from hospital rejoining unit)	App. A117
			Lt. Col. R. H. Johnston proceeded on leave. Major H. Pattinson in temporary command of the Bn.	App. A117
	9-2-16		Bn. in billets found working parties of 400 men.	App. A117
	10-2-16		Adjutant visited H.D. QHS 15 D.L.I. and saw subsidiary line which Bn. is to occupy 13/14 inst.	App. A117
	11-2-16		Bn. in billets; provision of working parties. Acting C/o and 2 Coy commanders attended course of Grenade work lectures demonstrations etc.	
			Adjutant 2 Coy commanders + 2 other officers with BS Mjr. + H-sergeants visited SUBSIDIARY LINE now held by 15 D.L.I. and reconnoitred.	
	12-2-16		Bn in billets ARMENTIÈRES lightly shelled	Appdx A117
	13-2-16		Bn. leaves "Battalion in support" moving to HOUPLINES and relieving 15 th DURHAMS.	
			2 Coys in SUBSIDIARY LINE and 2 in HOUPLINES. 1 casualty. 2nd Lts. CRAGG and ROWCROFT rejoined Batt.	
	14-2-16		Bn in support.	Appdx A117
				Appdx A117

Army Form C. 2118

WAR DIARY
or
INTELLIGENCE SUMMARY

(Erase heading not required.)

Instructions regarding War Diaries and Intelligence Summaries are contained in F. S. Regs., Part II. and the Staff Manual respectively. Title Pages will be prepared in manuscript.

Place	Date	Hour	Summary of Events and Information	Remarks and references to Appendices
ARMENTIÈRES	15-2-16		Bⁿ in support	Appx. Rep⁷
"	16-2-16		Bⁿ became "Battalion in reserve" relieving 4TH MIDDLESEX — quartered at TISSAGE, HOUPLINES	Appx. Rep⁷
"	17-2-16		Bⁿ in reserve. 2nd Lt. ALLBONES joined Bⁿ. DCT Rep⁷ Drafts returned up to date	Appx. Rep⁷
"	18-2-16		Bⁿ in reserve	Appx. Rep⁷
"	19-2-16		Bⁿ in reserve	Appx. Rep⁷
"	20-2-16		Bⁿ relieved 8TH SOMERSETS in trenches at 3-0 a.m. Disposition: Trenches 79 (from EPINETTE ROAD) and 75, No 2 Coy. Trenches 79 and 80, No 1 Coy. Trenches 81, 82, 83 (to PETTY CURY) No 4 Coy. Subsidiary line No 3 Coy.	Appx. Rep⁷
"	21-2-16		Bⁿ in trenches	Appx. Rep⁷
"	22-2-16		Bⁿ in trenches	Appx. Rep⁷
"	23-2-16		Bⁿ in trenches. Bⁿ H.Q. SUBSIDIARY LINE, Trenches 78, 79, 80 heavily bombarded. Casualties 9 (2 killed 7 wounded)	Appx. Rep⁷
"	24-2-16		Bⁿ in trenches. Much activity at night; our artillery having shelled parts of enemy line including portion opposite trench 79 (PONT BALLOT SALIENT) in morning opened very fire upon at night. Very little retaliation and Lt. CRAGG sick to	Appx. Rep⁷
"	25-2-16		FIELD AMBULANCE. Bⁿ in trenches relieved at 8.30 p.m. by 12ᵀᴴ NORTHUMBERLAND FUSILIERS and proceeded to billets in ARMENTIÈRES.	Appx. Rep⁷
"	26-2-16		Bⁿ in billets. Lieut LAFFERTY joined the Bⁿ	Appx. Rep⁷

Army Form C. 2118

WAR DIARY
or
INTELLIGENCE SUMMARY
(Erase heading not required.)

Instructions regarding War Diaries and Intelligence Summaries are contained in F. S. Regs., Part II. and the Staff Manual respectively. Title Pages will be prepared in manuscript.

Place	Date	Hour	Summary of Events and Information	Remarks and references to Appendices
ARMENTIÈRES	27-2-16		Bn in billets – 1 casualty (wounded on wiring party)	Appx A.1
	28-2-16		Bn in billets	Appx B.1
	29-2-16		Bn in billets – 3 casualties (wounded) O.R. 878	Appx C.1
			Strength of Bn 34 Officers	
			R.W.L. Smith Lt Col. Cmdg 1st Lincolnshire Regt	

1875 Wt. W593/826 1,000,000 4/15 J.B.C. & A. A.D.S.S./Forms/C. 2118.

8th (Serv) Bn. Lincolnshire Regt

Reinforcements arrived during the month of February 1916

Date	Officers	Other Ranks
7th	—	49
13th	2/Lt. Cragg J.F. 2/Lt. Rowcroft W.G.	
16th		1
17th	2/Lt. Allbones F.W.	
19th		5
26th	2/Lt. Lafferty G.G.	

1/3/16.

R.H. Johnston Lt. Col
Cmdg. 8th Bn. Lincolnshire

8th (Service) The Lincolnshire Regiment.

Casualties for the month of February 1916

	Through Sickness	Wounded	Killed
In billets and on Working Parties	24	10	Nil
In trenches	5	11	3

Offrs: — 2/Lt. Cragg J.T. Sick to Hospital 25-2-16
2/Lt. Grossman F.L. Reported sick on leave in England 23/2/16
2/Lt. Hawthorn E.G. — do — 22/6

R.M. Johnston Lt. Col.
Cmdg. 8th Bn. Lincolnshire Regt.

1/3/16.

Army Form C. 2118

WAR DIARY
or
INTELLIGENCE SUMMARY
(Erase heading not required.)

8 lines/cols

Place	Date	Hour	Summary of Events and Information	Remarks and references to Appendices
ARMENTIÈRES	1-3-16		Bn in billets	Sml Rxn
	2-3-16		Bn relieved 1st E. YORKSHIRE Rgt in Trenches - right sector. No 1 Coy - T67 x 68 / No 4 Coy T68 x 69 / No 3 Coy T70 x MUSHROOM / No 2 Coy LILLE POST	Sml Rxn
	3-3-16		Bn in Trenches - 70 Trench heavily shelled.	Sml Rxn
	4-3-16		Bn in Trenches. Arrived reinforcement 30 men + 3 N.C.O's.	Sml Rxn
	5-3-16		Bn in Trenches - one man killed. No 2 Coy moved to T70 & MUSHROOM. No 3 Coy moved to LILLE POST	Sml Rxn
	6-3-16		Bn in Trenches	Sml Rxn
	7-3-16		Bn in Trenches - one man killed. Capt. JONES wounded. Lt. B.A. Beard assumed command of No 2 Coy and 8-3-16	Sml Rxn / Sml Rxn
	8-3-16		Bn moved to Subsidiary line & SPY - SPY - PORTE EGAL REDOUBT. Relieved by 10th YORK. & LANCS. Regt.	Sml Rxn / Sml Rxn
	9-3-16		Bn in Subsidiary Line	
	10-3-16		Bn in Subsidiary Line. Captain E. M. Harrison joined Bn from 9th Res. Bn.	Sml Rxn
	11-3-16		Bn relieved by 4th MIDDLESEX Regt. Bn became Reserve Bn & moved to billets in ARMENTIÈRES	Sml Rxn
	12-3-16		Bn in billets	Sml Rxn
	13-3-16		Bn in billets. Arrived reinforcement 20 men	Sml Rxn
	14-3-16		Bn relieved 4th MIDDLESEX Regt of Subsidiary Line. A & B Company in Subsidiary Line. 8 SOMERSET LIGHT INFANTRY at T72 x 73 - 10th YORK & LANCASTERS C in Trenches 72 x 73 & D Company T70. 2 Lt. S. PHILLIPPS wounded	Sml Rxn
	15-3-16		Bn in Trenches. Lt. Bartley killed - 2/Lt. R.B. Lowe killed. 2 men wounded	Sml Rxn
	16-3-16		Bn in Trenches. 3 men wounded - 2 men killed	Sml Rxn
	17-3-16		Bn in Trenches. Visit of Lt General Ferguson Commanding 2nd Corps to Trenches. Four men wounded.	Sml Rxn

WAR DIARY
or
INTELLIGENCE SUMMARY
(Erase heading not required.)

Army Form C. 2118

Instructions regarding War Diaries and Intelligence Summaries are contained in F.S. Regs., Part II. and the Staff Manual respectively. Title Pages will be prepared in manuscript.

Place	Date	Hour	Summary of Events and Information	Remarks and references to Appendices
	18-3-16		Bn in Trenches. 1 man wounded.	Sml Rpt
	19-3-16		Bn in Trenches. 3 wounded by a premature from our own artillery - Lt F.E.C. Fairweather killed by sniper.	Sml Rpt
	20-3-16		Bn relieved in Trenches by 8th South Staffordshire Regt - 17th Division and moved to billets in ARMENTIÈRES.	Sml Rpt
	21-3-16		Bn in billets.	Sml Rpt
	22-3-16		Bn moved by road from ARMENTIÈRES to STEENWERCK & billets.	Sml Rpt
	23-3-16		Bn moved from STEENWERCK to billets in farms 2 3/4 mile N.E. of STRAZEELE. Lt Beard took command of No 4 Coy dated 16-3-16. 2Lt Rowcroft took Temp. Command of No 2 Coy dated 16-3-16.	Sml Rpt
	24-3-16		Bn in billets - Bn route march.	Sml Rpt
	25-3-16		Bn in billets -	Sml App
	26-3-16		Bn in billets -	Sml App
	27-3-16		Bn in billets - Transport inspected by Brigadier General Hill	Sml App
	28-3-16		Bn in billets - Bn marched past to General Sir Herbert Plumer GCom d'ing II Army Lieut. General Sir Charles Ferguson Comdg 2nd Corps	Sml App
	29-3-16		Bn in billets. Capt. Jones rejoined Bn	Sml App
	30-3-16		Bn in billets.	Sml App
	31-3-16		Bn entrained at GODEWAERSVELDE for LONGUEAU (S.E. of AMIENS) to join XIII Corps. * Marching out strength of Bn 25 officers 6 warrant officers 702 other ranks.	Sml App * Appendix IV

Roll of Officers in 8th Bn Lincolnshire Regt

Rank & Name	Coy Ration with	Date of Mobilie/3. Date 29/3/16	Date of Joining	Qualification & Remarks
Lieut Col R. H. Johnston D.S.O.	H.Q.		18. 11. 15.	Commanding
Major H. Pattinson	H.Q.	19. 9. 14.	19. 9. 14.	Second in Command
Capt. F. Brown	H.Q.	19. 12. 14.	19. 12. 14.	Adjutant
" R. A. Ker	H.Q.	22. 9. 14.	25. 9. 14.	Transport Officer
" E. M. Harrison	No 3		10. 3. 15.	Machine Gun Officer
Lieut E. M. Carre	No 3	3. 10. 15.	1. 11. 15.	Intelligence Sniping Off.
" S. Ferry	No 1.	4. 1. 15.	9. 10. 15.	Bn Grenadier Offr.
Lt & Qr Mr F. Taylor	H.Q.	10. 3. 15.	10. 3. 15.	
2nd Lieut F. W. Allbones	No 1.		17. 2. 16.	Signalling Off.

No. 1 Company

Lieut E. R. Devonshire	No 1.	26. 1. 15.	13. 10. 15.	O. C. Company
" F. W. Latham	No 1.	24. 4. 15.	6. 10. 15.	Platoon Com'd Billeting Off.
2nd Lieut C. W. Rhodes	No 1.	3. 10. 15.	3. 11. 15	- do - Coy Grenadier Off.

No. 2 Company

Capt. A. C. Jones		3. 10. 15.	1. 11. 15.	O. C. Company
2nd Lieut M. G. Rowcroft	No 2.	22. 12. 14.	13. 2. 16.	Actg O. C. Company
" L. D. Edwards		16. 9. 14.	9. 10. 15.	Att 63/2 T. M. Battery
" A. Lill	No 2.	25. 2. 15.	13. 10. 15.	Platoon Com'dr
" E. B. Markham		27. 3. 15	13. 10. 15.	- do - Grenadier Off.

No 3 Company

Capt. R. G. Cordiner	No 3.	20. 9. 14.	20. 9. 14.	O. C. Company
Lieut C. D. Jessopp	No 3.	22. 9. 14.	13. 10. 15.	Platoon Com'd Grenadier Off.
" R. A. Preston	No 3.	24. 4. 15.	6. 10. 15.	- do - - do -
2nd Lieut E. A. Duff	No 3.	2. 5. 15.	6. 10. 15.	- do - - do -

No 4 Company

Lieut B. J. L. Beard	No 4.	11. 2. 15.	13. 10. 15.	O. C. Company
2nd Lieut F. S. Boadle	No 4.	2. 11. 14.	9. 10. 15.	Platoon Com'dr
" W. H. Stephens		21. 1. 15.	9. 10. 15.	Att 182nd Tunnelling Coy
" R. L. Courtice	No 4.	16. 1. 16.	21. 1. 16.	Platoon Com'd Grenadier Off.
" W. F. Haward	No 4	16. 1. 16.	21. 1. 16.	- do -
" G. G. Lafferty	No 4.	2. 9. 16.	26. 2. 16.	- do -

F. Brown Capt & Adjutant
8th (Serv.) Bn. Lincolnshire Regiment.

APPENDIX IV

Operation Orders   No 25   by
Lieut Col. R.H. Johnston   D.S.O.
Commanding 8th Batt. Lincolnshire Regiment
Thursday 30th March 1916.

30. Move. The Battalion will entrain at GODEWAERSVELDE tomorrow night 31st inst. at 9-55 P.M.

31. Entraining Party. No 1 Company and Transport will arrive at GODEWAERSVELDE STATION at 7-55 P.M. leaving their billets here at 5-20 P.M. (Dress – Full Marching Order) and will load all baggage on the train under orders of Major H. Pattinson. No troops or transport will enter GODEWAERSVELDE STATION yard until the R.T.O. gives permission.

32. Time of Parade & Rendezvous. Bn will form up in column of route facing WEST along the road just North of No. 1 and 3 Coy's billets in the following order No 3 Coy. No 2 Coy. No 4 Coy. H.Q. Coy. The rear of No. 3 Coy and the head of No 2 Coy will be opposite to the entrance gate to the billet field at 7 P.M.

33. Guides. The guides previously sent on today 30th inst will march at the head of No 3 Coy but without their bicycles.

34. Rearguard. One Officer and four men per Company will see that the billets are perfectly clean before marching off. They will then form a rearguard immediately behind the Battalion and bring along all men who fall out. They will fall in, in rear of the Battalion and report "all present" before the Battalion marches off.

35. Falling out in line of march. All men falling out must be brought along by the rearguard. One Officer must march behind each company. No man must fall out without a written pass from an Officer to the Medical Officer who will be in rear of the Battalion.
All bicycles will be handed over to the O/C Rearguard.

36. Coy Marching out states. Coy marching out states must be sent to Adjutant at 12 noon tomorrow 31st inst.

37. Train Pickets. A guard of N.C.O. and 6 men at each end of the train will be found by the Coy's occupying the end carriages. At each stop these guards will find two sentries each one on each side of the train who will stand on the ground alongside the train and prevent any man from going away.

38. Salvage in billets. Any salvage found in billets should be collected before troops leave billets, and brought to Quarter Master Stores.

39. Blankets etc. Waterproof sheets and blankets will be rolled in bundles of twenties ready to load on the lorries at 5-45 P.M.

41. Guide for lorries. The two guides who met the lorries before will be detailed by Major H. Pattinson to meet the two lorries at STRAZEELE CHURCH at 5-50 P.M.
These lorries will be brought to the Quarter Master stores first.

42. Haversack Ration. Waterbottles will be carried – full.
Bread, Bacon, Cheese and Chocolate will be issued by Quarter Master to Coys at time to be arranged by O/C Coys and Qr Master.

43. Advance Party. The Blankets & the surplus of No 1 Coy should be sent to Quarter Master's Stores by 4 p.m.

To. –   No 1 Copy   H.Q. Coy   No 8 Copy
2nd in Command " 2 "   Transport Officer   " 9   "
Adjutant   " 3 "   Quarter Master   " 10 "
O/C No 1 Coy   " 4 "   Medical Officer   " 11 "
O/C No 2 Coy   " 5 "   Machine Gun Officer " 12 "
O/C No 3 Coy   " 6 "   Signalling Officer " 13 "
O/C No 4 Coy   " 7 "   Grenadier Officer No 14 by

F. Brown Capt. Adjt.
8th Bn Lincolnshire

8th (RESV) Bn. LINCOLNSHIRE REGIMENT

Nominal Roll of Officers passing forth until 30th April 1916.

Rank	Name	Employment	Date of Joining	Training
Lt. Col.	R. H. Johnston D.S.O.	Commanding Officer	15 – 11 – 15	Musketry Course HYTHE. STAFF COLLEGE COURSE.
Major	H. Pattinson	Second in Command	19 – 9 – 14	STAFF COLLEGE COURSE.
Capt.	J. Brown	Adjutant	19 – 12 – 14	M. G. Course HYTHE.
"	E. Th. Harrison	M. G. Officer	10 – 3 – 15	Course at ABBEVILLE.
"	R. A. Kerr	Transport Officer	29 – 9 – 14	A. G. + RANGE FINDING.
"	R. G. Codner	2/c No. 3 Coy.	20 – 9 – 14	STAFF COLLEGE COURSE.
"	F. C. Halston	Second 2/c No. 1 Coy.	24 – 4 – 16	
"	R. E. Bromohie	2/c No. 1 Coy.	13 – 10 – 15	
"	J. C. Jones	2/c No. 2 "	1 – 11 – 15	
Lt.	R. A. Preston	Platoon Commander. Asst Adjt Offr	6 – 10 – 15	2nd ARMY. GRENADE COURSE. TERDEGHEM.
"	C. R. Jossett	Platoon Commander. Coy. Bombing Offr	13 – 10 – 15	21st DIV. GRENADE SCHOOL.
"	B. K. Beard	Acting Bde. Major 63rd Bde.	13 – 10 – 15	M. G. Course in ENGLAND.
"	S. Ferry	Platoon Commander. Attached	9 – 10 – 15	2nd ARMY GRENADE COURSE TERDEGHEM.
"	M. Latham	Intelligence Officer. 4th Army Course	6 – 10 – 15	ATTENDING 4th ARMY COURSE AT FELIXCOURT.
"	E. M. Carr	Bn. Bombing Officer	1 – 11 – 15	21st DIV. GRENADE SCHOOL.
"	J. Taylor	Quartermaster	10 – 3 – 15	
Hon.				
Lt.	2/M Allbones	Signalling Officer	17 – 2 – 16	SIGNALLING COURSE OTLEY ENGLAND.
2Lt.	R. L. Contree	Platoon Commander. Coy. Bombing Offr	24 – 1 – 16	21st DIV. GRENADE SCHOOL.
"	A. J. Robbo Robbo	Platoon Commander. Coy. M.G. Offr	4 – 4 – 16	M. G. Course under Bn. M. G. Offr.
"	A. G. Rowroft	Act. 2/c No. 2 Coy. Coy. A. G. Officer.	13 – 2 – 16	"
"	H. Kill	Platoon Commander	13 – 10 – 15	21st DIV. GRENADE SCHOOL.
"	S. B. Markham	Platoon Commander. Coy Bombing Officer	13 – 11 – 15	
"	C. W. Rhodes	Platoon Commander. Coy M. G. Offr	3 – 11 – 15	
"	S. A. Duff	Platoon Commander	6 – 10 – 15	M. G. Course under Bn. M. G. Offr.
"	J. T. C. Baker	Platoon Commander	19 – 4 – 16	
"	G. G. Lafferty	Act. 2/c No. 7 Coy.	16 – 2 – 16	
"	J. S. Boadle	Platoon Commander Coy Bomb.g Officer.	9 – 10 – 15	
"	W. J. Howard	Platoon Commander. Coy M.G Officer.	24 – 1 – 16	
"	W. Swift	Platoon Commander	19 – 4 – 16	
"	J. J. Cass	Platoon Commander. G. M. G Officer.	13 – 2 – 16	M. G. Course HYTHE.
"	L. Edwards	Attached 63/2 L. F. M. B.	9 – 10 – 15	
"	W. H. Maples	" 183rd Tunnelling Coy.	9 – 10 – 15	

R. H. Johnston
Lt. Colonel.
Commdg. 8th (RESV) Bn. LINCOLNSHIRE REGT.

Army Form C. 2118

WAR DIARY
or
INTELLIGENCE SUMMARY
(Erase heading not required.)

Instructions regarding War Diaries and Intelligence Summaries are contained in F. S. Regs., Part II. and the Staff Manual respectively. Title Pages will be prepared in manuscript.

Place	Date	Hour	Summary of Events and Information	Remarks and references to Appendices
LONGEAU ALLONVILLE	1-4-16		Arrival at LONGEAU - Detrained. Marched to ALLONVILLE via AMIENS. Arrival at ALLONVILLE 1.20 p.m. Bn. in billets.	Appx
"	2.4.16		Bn. in billets. Bn. training carrying out work per C/o. Programme.	Appx
"	3.4.16		Bn. in billets. Bn. training carrying out route March. 6 miles training en route billets of the 1st Bn.	Appx
"	4.4.16		Bn. exercised in Route March. 6 miles training en route near billets.	Appx
"	5.4.16		Bn. in training on ground near billets.	Appx
"	6.4.16		Bn. in training; 10 men per coy. allowed leave into AMIENS. Work done in making skeleton trench using entrenching	Appx
"	7.4.16		Bn. in training. Bn. exercised in praying distances. implements. Operation Order No. 38 received. 63rd Bde. HQ moved to VILLE. Bde Operation order published. Arrangements made for the move to BUIRE. Bn. Operation order published.	Appx
"	8.4.16		On the Bttn net. Bn. paraded at 8.30 A.M. in the quadrangle of the farm in billets. Marching out Strength. Bn. halted and had dinner en route. 22 Officers 6 Warrant Officers 668 Other Ranks.	Appx
BUIRE.	8.4.16		Bn. arrived in BUIRE and billeted here 2.30 p.m.	Appx
"	9.4.16		Bn. in training in billets; working party of 200 other ranks and 5 officers found for 110th Rly Coy. R.E.	Appx
"	10.4.16		Bn. in billets. No. 1 Coy. trained in all day bombing Course under Bde. Grenadier Officer.	Appx

WAR DIARY
or
INTELLIGENCE SUMMARY

(Erase heading not required.)

Army Form C. 2118

Place	Date	Hour	Summary of Events and Information	Remarks and references to Appendices
BUIRE	11.4.16		Bn in billet. Training carried out	Appx. Rep
	12.4.16		Bn in billet. Training carried out	Appx. Rep
	13.4.16		Bn in billet. No 2 Coy trained under Bde. Grenadier Officer in one days course of Bombing. Fatigue Party 200 men found for 110th Rly. Coy. R.E.	Appx.
	14.4.16		Bn moved into Bn. in support - (1st Middlesex + 8th Somersets L.I. occupying front line) No. 3 Coy in QUEEN'S REDOUBT. No 4 Coy in BONTE REDOUBT. No. 1 + 2 Coy in BONTE BECORDEL village. Bn. HdQrs in MEAULTE.	Appx. Rep
			No. 1 + 2 Coy furnish fatigue parties for Mining Operations on RIGHT SECTOR. 2 Lt Markham rejoined Bn. from hospital.	Appx.
MEAULTE	15.4.16		A few shells sent into MEAULTE by enemy, otherwise situation normal. 1st Buff + tatters under Course of Instruction in M.G. Officer. Casualties 2 men seriously, 5 other men slightly (one since dead) 16.4.16.	Appx Rep
"	16.4.16		Enemy position in MAMETZ bombarded. 3 p.m. Casualties 1 man killed 2 severely wounded, 1 slightly wounded.	Appx Rep
"	17.4.16		A somewhat quiet day. No 4 Coy reveived working party of 101 men 7th Regt for building trench. one man died of wounds no 5 C.C.S.	Appx
"	18.4.16		No 4 Coy with fatigue party 7th Regt. completed LINDUM ST. HdQrs. occupied trenches in left sector.	Appx
"	19.4.16		Coy under Capt. H.C. Jones with 110th. 1 man killed 1 man wounded.	Appx
"	20.4.16		Enemy shelled MEAULTE. Casualties in BONTE + QUEEN'S REDOUBT + BECORDEL Reserve Rations checked.	Appx
"	21.4.16		Officers from 12 N.F. visited BONTE + QUEEN'S REDOUBT to reconnoitre - preparatory to taking over. Operation order 28 published.	Appx
"	22.4.16		Bn. handing to BUIRE being relieved in trenches (as Bn in support) by 12 Northumberland Fusiliers. Bn arrived in BUIRE 4 p.m. Bn received orders to move to La NEUVILLE - leaving BUIRE as soon as possible.	Appx
La NEUVILLE			Bn. arrived in LA NEUVILLE (nr CORBIE) at 8.30 p.m.	Appx

WAR DIARY
or
INTELLIGENCE SUMMARY

Army Form C. 2118

(Erase heading not required.)

Place	Date	Hour	Summary of Events and Information	Remarks and references to Appendices
LA NEUVILLE	23.4.16		Bn. in billets. Rifles and ammunition cleaned. 1 Coy. bathed.	M.Pm?
"	24.4.16		Bn. found working party of 11 Officers and 500 men.	M.Pm?
"	25.4.16		Bn. in billets. Bn. bathed. Smoke helmets of 2 Coys inspected by gas expert.	M.Pm?
"	26.4.16		Working party of 11 Officers and 500 men found.	M.Pm?
"	27.4.16		Bn. practised in attack over trenches; No. 3 Coy trained in one day Grenade course.	M.Pm?
"	28.4.16		Bn. in billets. Training carried out.	M.Pm?
"	29.4.16		Bn. in billets. Training carried out. Exercise in Intrenching.	M.Pm?
"	30.4.16		Bn. CHURCH PARADE. Commanding Officer took Off. Companies and 2/C. M.G. Bombers and Signallers to reconnoitre ground for Bn. attack exercise to take place on 1st MAY.	M.Pm?

Operation Orders No 26 by
Lieut Col R. H. Johnston D.S.O.
Commanding 8th/(S) Bn Lincolnshire Regt
Thursday April 6th 1916

1. Move. The Battalion will march to BUIRE (12 miles) on the morning of the 8th inst.

2. Order of March. H.Q. Coy., No 4 Coy., No 3 Coy., No 2 Coy., No 1 Coy., Transport & Rear Guard.

3. Breakfast. 7-15 A.M.

4. Parade. Battalion will parade in full marching order in farm quadrangle ready to march off at 8-30 A.M.

5. Dinners. Battalion will march via PONT NOYELLES along main AMIENS – ALBERT Road. The cookers will cook on the march and go ahead to where the FRANVILLERS – HEILLY Road crosses this road where Battalion will halt for dinners.
Officers will make their own arrangements to have lunch on the road.

6. Blankets. Blankets and waterproof sheets will be rolled in bundles of twenty ready to be loaded at 6-45 A.M. 8th inst.

7. Motor Lorries. The same two guides who met lorries before will be detailed by the Adjutant to meet two lorries at ALLONVILLE CHURCH at 6-50 A.M. 8th inst and bring them to Bn billets.

8. Rear Guard. One officer and four men per Company including H.Q. Coy will see that all billets are clean by 8-30 A.M. 8th inst. These 20 men and an Officer each from No 1 and H.Q. Coy will then form rear-guard marching off with the Bn immediately behind transport and will bring along all stragglers.
All bicycles not used by the billeting party will be handed over to the Officer in charge of rear guard at 7-30 A.M. 8th inst.

9. Waterproof Capes. Waterproof capes will be carried inside pack.

10. Dress Men may either wear the pack in the regulation way, in which case, during ordinary halts, the packs must not be taken off, but the belt may be undone, and men lay back on their packs. Or they may wear the packs separate from the equipment slung over the shoulders by coat straps, in which case the packs may be taken off during halts.

11. Billeting Party Lieut F. W. Latham and same billeting party as before, will meet A/Staff Captain (Lieut Thorne) at BUIRE CHURCH at 10 A.M. 8th inst.

12. Damages. All damage books will be completed and a report forwarded to the Adjutant that this has been done by 7 A.M. 8th inst.

13. Marching Out States. Marching out states will be sent in to the Adjutant by 12 noon tomorrow – 7th instant.

F. Brown Capt & Adjt
8th/Serv/Bn Lincolnshire Regt

SECRET

Operation Orders by
Lieut Col R. H. Johnston. D.S.O.
Commanding 8th Bn Lincolnshire Regiment.
Thursday 13th April 1916

1. Move — The Battalion will relieve the 10th Batt K.O.Y.L.I. in QUEENS REDOUBT (1 Company) BONTE REDOUBT (1 Company) and BECORDEL BECOURT village (2 Companies), Bn Headquarters in MEAULTE on afternoon of the 14th instant.

2. Disposition — No 4 Coy in QUEENS REDOUBT.
" 3 " " BONTE
Nos 2 & 1 Coys BECORDEL Village.

3. Forward Party — One Officer and one N.C.O. per company will leave here at 9 A.M. 14th inst and take over stores and find out all details, remaining in position which their company will occupy, except the Officer and N.C.O. of No 1 and No 2 Coys who will arrange with Lieut Latham as to guides for companies.

4. Guides — For No 1 & 2 Coys as above.
Machine Gun Officer, Signalling Officer, Bombing Officer, Pioneer Sgt, and Headquarters will send two guides, each to Lieut Latham at MEAULTE Church at 10-30 P.M. 14th inst.

5. Motor Lorry — Quarter Master will detail one guide to meet one lorry at 7 A.M. 14th inst at VILLE Church and bring it to billets.
Bn Sergt Major will proceed on this lorry to MEAULTE.

6. Blankets — Blankets will be rolled in twenty's ready to be loaded on lorries at 7 A.M. 14th inst.

7. Waterproof Sheets — will be carried on the man.

8. Order of March. — No 4   No 3   No 2   No 1   H.Qrs.
Coys will march from billet by platoons at 300 yards interval. Leading platoon of No 4 Coy to pass BUIRE Church at 12.45 p.m. 14th inst and march via DERNANCOURT passing MEAULTE Church at 2.30 p.m. 14th inst.

9. Dinners — Dinner at 11-30 A.M. 14th inst. Orders re cookers will be issued later.

10. Transport — Transport and Qtr Mtr Stores will remain at BUIRE.

11. Mac Gun. — 2 Machine Guns and teams will be sent to 4th Middlesex. M.G. Officers of both units to arrange details.

12. Mining Fatigues — Mining Fatigues will be found by No 1 & 2 Coys commencing at 6 p.m. 14th inst with No 1 Company. No 2 Coy taking over their duties at 6 A.M. 15th inst and so on.
Copy of Mining Fatigues Orders is attached herewith. No 1 Coy to note and hand to No 2 Coy.

13. Reports — When Companies and detachments are in new billets they will report to that effect to Headquarters.

14. Baggage — Surplus baggage and mess kit to be ready packed and labelled at Officers' billet by 12.15 p.m. 14th inst.
Officers' Baggage to be ready by 11 a.m. 15th inst.

F. Brown Capt. Adjt.
8th Batt Lincolnshire Regiment

Army Form C. 2118

WAR DIARY or INTELLIGENCE SUMMARY

(Erase heading not required.)

2/143
8 Lincolns
Vol. 8

Place	Date	Hour	Summary of Events and Information	Remarks and references to Appendices
La NEUVILLE	1-5-16		BN. paraded for ROUTE MARCH at 9 A.M. Returned to billets 12-45 P.M.	
	2-5-16		BN. became Divisional Support. Q Coys in MEAULTE. H.Q col. & others in MEAULTP.	
MEAULTE	3-5-16		BN. Divisional Support. Head Quarters & others in VILLE. H.coe. & others in MEAULTE	HP
"	4-5-16		" " " "	HP
"	5-5-16		" " " " 1. C.S.M. Clifford wounded.	HP
"	6-5-16		" " " Corporal Rawton wounded	HP
"	7-5-16		" " " 2 O.R. Leavers returned from T.M. Battery	HP
"	8-5-16		" " "	HP
"	9-5-16		" " " Working parties found Bde in line	HP
"	10-5-16		" " " "	HP
"	11-5-16		" " " "	HP
"	12-5-16		BN. relieved 15 D.L.I. in right sector of line. No. 1. occupied right No. 3 Coy centre and No. 2 and 4 Coy occupied supports and TAMBOUR each coy in line 3 days. 4 wounded. and 1 killed.	HP
"	13-5-16		BN. in line trenches shelled 1 killed 6 wounded	HP
"	14-5-16		Bn in line quiet day.	HP
"	15-5-16		Bn in line 1 wounded.	HP
"	16-5-16		Bn in line 1 killed 2 wounded.	HP
"	17-5-16		Bn in line generally quiet no casualties.	HP
"	18-5-16		Bn in line Divisional Comdr. visited HQrs. and munged round the trenches. Divisional Commander visited casualties 4 wounded trench shelled	HP
"	19-5-16		Lt. Col. R.H. Johnston D.S.O on leave. usual enemy strafing 8-9 P.M. our retaliation effective. casualties 1 man killed, Tranfant wounded.	HP
"	20-5-16		BN. in line a quiet day 1 man died of wounds.	HP
"	21-5-16		Bn in line. Officers of 1st Mr. Lincolnshire visited trenches preparatory to taking over on	HP

WAR DIARY
or
INTELLIGENCE SUMMARY

Army Form C. 2118

(Erase heading not required.)

Place	Date	Hour	Summary of Events and Information	Remarks and references to Appendices
VILLE	22/5/16		Bn relieved in left sector by pt. Bn. Lincolnshire Regt. Bn marched into VILLE and billeted the night of the 22nd there.	7/13.
	23/5/16		Bn. paraded at 6-30 A.M. and marched to La NEUVILLE. into rest billets.	7/13.
LA NEUVILLE	24/5/16		Bn. in rest. Scheme of training carried out No.1 Coy attack on trenches. Attended 5. The Corps Commander being present.	7/13.
"	25/5/16		Bn. in rest. Day spent in bathing the Bn. Refitting and setting up deficiencies.	7/13.
"	26/5/16		Bn. in rest. Training carried out Route march. Bn. Concert.	7/13.
"	27/5/16		Bn. in rest. No 1 Coy. Bombing Practice. Nos 2. 3. 4. Coys worked under scheme of work	7/13.
"	28/5/16		Bn. in rest. Attended Bde. Church Parade. Brig. Gen. will present.	7/13.
"	29/5/16		Bn. took part in Bde Exercise on trenches. Div. Gen. Major. Gen. Lt. M. Campbell C.M.G. 21st Div. and Brig. Gen'l. J. R. Hill C.M.G. 63rd Inf. Brigade present.	7/13.
"	30/5/16		Bn. in rest. Coys. exercised in Bombing No 1. Coy. 6-30 A.M. No 2 Coy 9 A.M No 3 Coy. 11 A.M. No. 4 Coy. 2 P.M.	7/13.
"	31/5/16		Bn. inspected by G.O.C. 21st DN. Major Genl. Lt. M. Campbell. First line transport inspected Bn. took part in Bde. Operations on trenches. Bde operation order received. Bn ordered to relieve 15th D.L.I. in BOIS DES TAILLES. Strength of Battalion fighting Strength. 911. Ration Str. 840 including Officers. Officers 31.	7/13.
"			Bn operation order issued. Appendix Lt.Col. R.H. Johnston D.S.O rejoined from leave. During Commanding Officers absence Major H. Patterson performed the duties y/o	7/13.

1875 W¹. W 593/826 1,000,000 4/15 J.R.C. & A. A.D.S.S./Forms/C. 2118.

8th Bn. Leinster Regiment   Programme of Work
Week 5

Day	7 – 7.30 a.m.	9 – 10.30 a.m.	11 – 12 noon	2 – 3 p.m.	Remarks
Wednesday 24th	Roll Call Physical drill	No 1 & 2 Coy practises attack over trenches. No 3 & 4 Coys shooting & Platoon Drill	No 1 & 2 Coy practises attack over trenches. No 3 & 4 Coys shooting & Platoon Drill	No 3 Coy rifle Inspection No 1 & 2 Coys Inspection of arms & ammunition by S.M. Armourer B.M. Drill	
Thursday 25th	Roll Call Physical drill and Bayonet fighting	— — — 1, 2 & 4 Coys	Bathes? — — — Rifle and clothing inspection	Coy Comdrs will inspect clothing under orders of Coy Sergt	Coy. London will inspect ESCARDINEUSE No 2
Friday 26th		4 hours march		Got Inspection	
Saturday 27th	Physical drill and Bayonet fighting	No 1 Coy. Bombing 2 Coy anti 3 Coy shooting 4 Coy anti	2 Coy shooting 3 Coy anti 4 Coy anti	Coys to be engaged under arrangements of Coy Comdrs Sports Athletic Sports	
Sunday 28th		Church Parade			
Monday 29th	Physical drill and Bayonet fighting	Bn. in attack over trenches	Bn. in attack over trenches	No 3 Coy at range No 4 Coy Rifle snipers at.	No 3 Coy Rifle Inspection
Tuesday 30th	— Do —	1 & 2 Coy Bn in attack over 3 & 4 Coy in Wood fighting Coy arries	1 & 2 Coy Bn in attack over 3 & 4 Coy in Wood fighting Coy arries	1 & 2 Coy Bn drill 3rd Coy throw attack trenches in Wood fighting	No 4 Coy Rifle inspection
Wednesday 31st	— Do —	1 Coy Platoon and 2 " Coy anti 3 " "	Section to men to Coy Offs Discipline	Bn in attack over trenches	
Thursday 1st	— Do —	Exercise in Wood fighting	Exercise in Wood fighting	All Coys in range an Snipers	

L. Brown Capt Fad.
Leicester Regt.

Appendix
 6.

```
        OPERATION   ORDERS    No 38   BY
       MAJOR   H.   P.ATTINSON,
           COMMDG. 8th LINCOLNSHIRE REGIMENT.
WEDNESDAY.      31st. May, 1916.
```

MOVE. Battalion will relieve 15th D.L.I. in BOIS DES TAILLES tomorrow the 1st June 1916.

BILLETING PARTY. Billeting party under Lieut. Carre will leave Battalion H.Q. at 12 noon 1st June 1916.

PARADE. Battalion will parade in full marching order ready to march off at 2-30.p.m. Steel helmets will be carried, but not worn. Battalion will form up in column of route facing S.W. as follows.

H.Q. Coy. No. 1 Coy. No. 2 Coy. in Rue de Eglise
No. 3. Coy. No. 4 Coy. in Rue de Marais.

ORDER OF MARCH.
H.Q. Coy.
No. 1 Coy.
No. 2 Coy.
No. 3. Coy.
No. 4. Coy.

REAR GUARD. 1 N.C.O. and 4 men per Coy. under 2/ Lt. R. L. Courtice will form rear-guard and will march in rear of transport.

BILLETs, All billets will be left scrupously clean, all rubbish will be collected by a wagon at 11 a.m. and taken to the incinerators. O. C. Coys will furnish written statement that the billets of officers and men have been inspected by them by 2 p.m. 1st June 1916.

BAGGAGE. All baggage, mess material etc. will be taken to Q.M. Stores by 1. 30 p.m. 1st June 1916.

F. Brown Capt & Adjut.

8th Lincolnshire Regiment.

"A" Form. Army Form C. 2121.
MESSAGES AND SIGNALS.

Prefix	Code	m.	Words	Charge	This message is on a/c of:	Recd. at	m.
Office of Origin and Service Instructions.			Sent			Date	
			At	m.	Service.	From	
			To				
			By		(Signature of "Franking Officer.")	By	

TO — Officer i/c Adjutant General's Office Base

| Sender's Number. | Day of Month | In reply to Number | | AAA |
| L7B 201 | 1st | | | |

9.15.	A7C 2118	forwarded herewith please
		J Brown Capt & Adj.
1/8/16		for O/c Lincolnshire Regt.

From
Place
Time
The above may be forwarded as now corrected. (Z)
Censor. Signature of Addressor or person authorised to telegraph in his name.
* This line should be erased if not required.

WAR DIARY or INTELLIGENCE SUMMARY

Army Form C.2118

Vol 9

Place	Date	Hour	Summary of Events and Information	Remarks and references to Appendices
La NEUVILLE	1-6-16		Bn. left La NEUVILLE at 2-30 p.m. and marched to BOIS DES TAILLES and took over camp formerly occupied by 1st Dn. Y.	2B. RM
BOIS DES TAILLES	2-6-16		Bn. arrived in camp at 7-5 p.m. Working party of 3 Officers and 300 men found by unit on the BRAY Railway.	2B. RM
"	2-6-16		Bn. found working parties:- 2 officers and 100 men at 8 A.M. } for work on " " 5 " 220 " 6-30 P.M. }	2B. RM
"	3-6-16		BRAY Railway. Bn. found working party of 2 Off and 100 NCOs and men at 8 A.M. and a similar party at 6 P.M. for work on Dn.	2B. RM
"	4-6-16		Bn. found working parties on Rly work of:- 20 Officers and 100 at 8 A.M. " " " " " " " 2 " 110 " 8 P.M. Transfer of Officers on M.G. (Lewis) carried on under 2. M. G. Officer. " " " " " Range finding " " " Adjt R.G. Cordiner. London Gazette "Honours List" Capt A.R. Jones awarded Military Cross No. 5536. Regt Q.M.S. (Act Sgn) P.H. Divane awarded Military Cross No 9327 Sgt C.J. Buckley awarded Military Medal. New NCOs. employed on working parties trained in Musketry.	2B. RM
"	5-6-16		Bn. employed in work on Rly near BRAY. Remainder trained in Musketry. Commanding Officer 2nd in Command, Coy. Commanders, Lewis M.G. Officer and Bombing Officer attended Conference at Bde. H.Q.	2B. RM
"	6-6-16		Bn. employed in work on Rly near BRAY.	
"	7-6-16		Bn. employed in work of Rly near BRAY. Enemy shelled road near Camp. Parties of 450 NCO's and men found. Officers of Coy engaged in Reconnaissance.	
"	8-6-16		Bn. employed in work on Rly near BRAY. Officers and Col. Major engaged in Reconnaissance. Coy. officers and Coy. Commanders engaged in Reconnaissance of area.	

Army Form C. 2118

WAR DIARY
or
INTELLIGENCE SUMMARY
(Erase heading not required.)

Instructions regarding War Diaries and Intelligence Summaries are contained in F. S. Regs., Part II. and the Staff Manual respectively. Title Pages will be prepared in manuscript.

Place	Date	Hour	Summary of Events and Information	Remarks and references to Appendices
BOIS DES TAILLES	9/6/16.		BN furnished working party of 50 NCOs and men for Rly. construction at BRAY. Training carried on with specialists under their officers. Proportion of officers did reconnaissance.	Appx. P.29
"	10/6/16.		BN in training. M. Gunners & Snipers trained as specialists. Bde. Op. Orders 55 received Adjutant went to MEAULTE to make arrangements as to relief of 1st Bn. EAST YORKSHIRE REGT. 9 Bn. K.O.Y.L.I. reported to take over camp at BOIS=des=TAILLES.	Appx. P.29
"	11/6/16.		Officers p.m. BN occupied in training during period 9am-12noon.	Appx. P.29
"	12/6/16.		Operation order 39 published re move to MEAULTE. BN. marched to MEAULTE via MORLANCOURT arrived W. end of MEAULTE at 4.15P.M. No 1 & 4 Coy. billeted on arrival. No 2 & 3 Coy. billeted when billets were evacuated in Meaut. Yorks at 9P.M. 2 & 3 Coy attached for working to 4th Middlesex & Somerset L.I. resp.	Appx. P.29
MEAULTE	13/6/16		BN. in Brigade Reserve. Working parties found for work on front defences.	Appx. P.29
"	13/6/16		BN in Brigade Reserve. Working parties found for work on front defences.	Appx. P.29
"	14.6.16.		BN. in Bde. Reserve. Working parties found for front line. Capt Kirstock on Bde Transport. 2nd Lt Rabson took over. No 2 Coy in Support trenches. Furnishing carrying parties to front line.	Appx. P.29
"	15.6.16		BN in Bde Reserve. Working Parties found for front defences. No 4 Coy occupied right sector.	Appx. P.29
"	16.6.16		BN relieved 4th Middlesex in right sector. No 1 Coy Supports. Quiet day 10 casualties. No 2 Coy centre. No 3 Coy in TAMBOUR.	Appx. P.29
"	17.6.16		Quiet day. BN in line. 10 casualties. Capt H.B. Dawes wounded.	Appx. P.29
"	18.6.16		BN in line. 2 wounded. Capt H.B. Dawes wounded from the 3rd Bedfords attached to Yorks.	Appx. P.29
"	19.6.16		BN in the line. The following officers arrived from the 9th Bn. 2nd Lt Parkin, 2nd Lt Walker 4th 2nd Lt Waugh F.A.	Appx. P.29

Army Form C. 2118

WAR DIARY
or
INTELLIGENCE SUMMARY
(Erase heading not required.)

Instructions regarding War Diaries and Intelligence Summaries are contained in F.S. Regs., Part II. and the Staff Manual respectively. Title Pages will be prepared in manuscript.

Place	Date	Hour	Summary of Events and Information	Remarks and references to Appendices
MEAULTE	20-6-16		Bn. relieved in right sector by 12 Northumberland Fusiliers marched to rest billets in LA NEUVILLE. Resting at VILLE for the night.	
LA NEUVILLE	21-6-16		At 9.30 p.m. Commanding Officer went to Conference at Bde. Bn. in rest billets. Refitting and making up deficiencies.	
"	22-6-16		Training carried out. Commanding Officer met officers of Bn. in Conference. Bn. in rest billets. Commanding Officer went to Conference at Bde. HQ.	
"	23-6-16		Bn. in rest billets. Practise over trenches carried. Commanding Officer went to Conference at Bde. HQ.	
"	24-6-16		Bn. took place in Bde. attack over trenches. Bde. Sports. Bn. had 1st average and aggregate 1st point in Bde.	
"	25-6-16		Bn. inspected by Divisional Commander Major-Genl. D. J. M. Campbell. Brig.Gen. E.R. Hill Cmdg. 63rd Inf. Bde. present.	
"	27-6-16		Bn. in billets. Training carried out.	
VILLE	28-6-16		Bn. left LA NEUVILLE for VILLE. 9 P.M. arrived at VILLE 1. 30 Am	
"	29-6-16		Bn. in billets.	
"	30-6-16		Bn. left VILLE for the trenches. – Being Bn. in support to 6 Somerset Light Infantry.	

War Diary

of

8th Bn. Lincolnshire Regiment

for

July 1916.

"A" Form.
MESSAGES AND SIGNALS

Army Form C. 2122.

Prefix	Code	Words	Charge	This message is on a/c of	Recd. at	m
Office of Origin and Service Instructions.		Sent		Service.	Date	
		At	m.		From	
		To		(Signature of "Franking Officer.")	By	
		By				

TO "Adjutant's General's Office

Sender's Number	Day of Month	In reply to Number	
27B 20	Thirty first		AAA

Herewith A.F.C. 2118 for July 1916.

From 8 Lincolnshire Regt
Place HQ.
Time 12 midnight.

R.H. Johnston Lt Col
Cmd 8 Lincolnshire R

WAR DIARY or INTELLIGENCE SUMMARY

Army Form C. 2118

JULY

Place	Date	Hour	Summary of Events and Information	Remarks and references to Appendices
VILLE	30/6/16	9.15	Bn. left VILLE for the trenches – Bn. in support left sector	O.O. 43 P.17 App. X P.17
TRENCHES	1/7/16		Bn. in attack in support to 8th Bn. SOMERSET LIGHT INFANTRY. Report upon operations and attack see Appendix by Cmd. Officer Lt. Col. R.H. Johnston D.S.O. Report upon medical arrangements during the attack by Capt. H.D. Schad R.A.M.C.	App. Y P.17
FRICOURT			Casualties. Officers killed 2/Lt J. Cragg, W. Swift, R.L. Curtice, J.H. Parkinson. Missing (believed killed & wounded) Capt. F.C. Jones. Officers wounded Capt. R.G. Cardew Lt. (temp Capt) G.R. Scamadine, Lt. G.G. Lafferty Lt. M.G. Rowcroft, 2/Lt. J.S. Bodle, W.J. Howard, E.G. Pritchell Other Ranks Killed 30 Wounded 197. Missing 12. Total O.R. Casualties 239.	2/8 P.17
	4.7.16.		Bn. relieved in the trenches and rested at DERNANCOURT where it entrained for AILLY sur SOMME and marched to VAUX-en-AMIENOIS	2/9. P.17
DERNANCOURT	4.7.16.		Bn. rested in billets	
VAUX	5.7.16 } 6-7.16 }			2 P.17
TALMAS	7.7.16		Bn. marched to TALMAS and billeted there. (3rd Bde. transferred to 37th Division)	2/5 P.17
	8.7.16		Bn " " MONDICOURT and billeted.	2/3 P.17
MONDICOURT	10.7.16		Commanding Officer and Coy. Commanders visited the trenches at HANNESCAMPS	2/5 P.17
"	11.7.16		Bn moved to the Trenches and relieved 5th Bn. LINCOLNSHIRE REGT. No.1 Coy in right No.2 Coy. in left and No 3 4th Coy in support at Bn. H.Q.	2/9 P.17
HANNESCAMPS	11-7.16 } 14.7.16 }		Bn. in trenches front line shelled lightly. 1 man wounded	2/3. P.17

WAR DIARY
or
INTELLIGENCE SUMMARY
(Erase heading not required.)

Army Form C. 2118

Instructions regarding War Diaries and Intelligence Summaries are contained in F.S. Regs., Part II. and the Staff Manual respectively. Title Pages will be prepared in manuscript.

Place	Date	Hour	Summary of Events and Information	Remarks and references to Appendices
TRENCHES	14-7-16		Bn. relieved in the trenches by the 2nd LONDON REGT.	See App.
HUMBERCAMP	15-7-16		Bn. billeted for night 14/15 at HUMBERCAMP.	See App.
			Bn. left HUMBERCAMP for HOUVIN, HOUVIGNEUL	See App.
HOUVIN	16-7-16		Bn. left HOUVIN and marched to BAILLEUL aux CORNAILLES and billeted there	See App.
	17-7-16		Bn. in billets. Reinforcement of officers 2/Lt T.R. Carter, R.G. Godfrey G.H. Smard from 3rd Bn. Lincolnshire Regt.	See App.
CAMBLAIN L'ABBE	18-7-16		Bn. moved to CAMBLAIN L'ABBE.	
	19-7-16		Bn. in training.	
"	20-7-16		Bn. reviewed by Divisional Commander 37th Div. Major Gen. Count Gleichen K.C.V.O.	See App.
			C.B. C.M.G. D.S.O. Reinforcement of 1 Officer 2Lt C.F.M. LILLEY	
"	21-7-16		Bn. in training. Re-equipping.	See App.
"	22-7-16		Bn. in training. Re-equipping. Was programme of work	See App.
			S.M.	
"	23-7-16		Bn. in training. Re-equipping.	See App.
"	24-7-16		Commanding Officer and Company Commanders visited trenches in	See App.
			support BERTHONVAL sub-section. Received Bde. O.O. 70.	See O.O. 61
			Bn. O.O. 61 published. Bn. relieved 8th Bn. LONDON REGT. in BERTHONVAL SECTION.	See O.O. 70
TRENCHES	25-7-16		Bn. in trenches.	See App.
"	26-7-16		Bn. in trenches. Reinforcement of 3 Officers 206 other Ranks. 2 Lt. Dukes S.H., Lloyd W.H., 2Lt.	See App.
"	27-7-16		Busher H.J.B.	
"	28-7-16		Bn. in trenches.	
"	29-7-16		Bn. in trenches. Reinforcement of two officers 2/Lt Read J. Serge A.J. from 11th Bn. Linc R.R.	
"	30-7-16		Bn. " " one other 2/Lt W.A. Keeling.	R.W. Johnson
"	31-7-16		Bn. " Took over trenches relieved 10th Bn. York Lancashire Regt.	Lt. Col.
				Cmdg. 8th Lincolnshire Regt.

1875 Wt. W593/826 1,000,000 4/15 J.B.C. & A. A.D.S.S./Forms/C. 2118.

OPERATION ORDERS NO. 43   SECRET
BY LIEUT. COL. R. H. JOHNSTON, D.S.O.
COMMANDING 8th BATTALION LINCOLNSHIRE REGIMENT.
SUNDAY. 25th JUNE, 1916.

ATTACK BY 15th CORPS.

1. Ultimate objective
   (a) 7th Division to capture MAMETZ, and occupy line S 25.B 5.3 to X 29.B 5.6.
   (b) 21st Division (with 50th Brigade attached) X 29 B 5.6 to trench junction X 22 B 6.7.
   (c) 34th Division will take CONTALMAISON.
   (note the clearing of FRICOURT and FRICOURT WOOD is being undertaken as a separate operation after the main attack has progressed)

2. FINAL OBJECTIVE.   64th Brigade junction of new trench and Quadrangle trench X 23 C 4.5. inclusive along Quadrangle trench to trench junction X 22 B 6.7. with posts in advance of this trench.

3. 63rd BRIGADE.   First objective.
   (a) 4th Middlesex Regiment - FRICOURT FARM X 28 C 8.7. - bend of trench at X 28 a 5.0.0.5 inclusive with advanced posts in RAILWAY ALLEY and COPSE up to RAILWAY LINE about X 28 B.1.3½ inclusive.
   8th Somerset L.I. bend of trench at X 28 a.5.0.0.5 exclusive CRUCIFIX TRENCH to X 27 B.7.8.4.1 with advanced posts from X 28.b.1.3. exclusive to S. end of SHELTER WOOD exclusive.
   (b) Second objective.
   10th York & Lancs. Regt. X 29 B 5.6 (joining 7th Division) thence along N edge of BOTTOM WOOD by works 16 and 17 the new trench entering BOTTOM WOOD at X 29 A 1.3 and along new trench to QUADRANGLE X 23 C 4.5 exclusive. point. X29. a 5.6½
   The following advanced lines will be occupied at once and consolidated as soon as main objective has been consolidated.
   63rd Brigade X 29.B.5.6. works 17 in QUADRANGLE WOOD to work 18 X 23 d.p.5.4 8 inclusive
   8th Lincolnshire Regt.
   X 29 A 50.65 in close touch with 10th Y. & L. Regt. along N. edge of BOTTOM WOOD thence along new trench to its junction with QUADRANGLE TRENCH about X 23 C 4.5. exclusive with advanced posts on the line X 23 d 1.0. works 17 and work 18 the line of advanced posts will be occupied at once and consolidated as rapidly as possible.

4. RESERVE. (a) 62nd. Brigade will form Divisional Reserve.
   Headquarters QUEENS REDOUBT.
   (b) 400 men of 62nd Brigade will act as carriers for 63rd. Brigade.

5. **ASSEMBLY TRENCH.** 63rd Bde. H. Qrs. at junction of 101 St. & SHUTTLE LANE

   8th. Linc. R. H.Qrs. junction of MARISCHAL and STONEHAVEN Streets.

   A Coy. in SHUTTLE LANE from junction of 104a St. to HUNTLEY ST.
   D Coy. in SHUTTLE LANE from junction of HUNTLEY STREET to STONEHAVEN.
   C Coy. in MARISCHAL St. from Queens AV. to HUNTLEY ST.
   B Coy. in MARISCHAL ST. from HUNTLEY ST. to 100 yards S. of STONEHAVEN St

   From left of "B" Coy. to STONEHAVEN from right to left, Rifle Grenadiers, Stretcher bearers, Battalion Grenadiers, Orderlies, Signallers.

6. **CLEARING UP COMPANY.** D Coy. will follow immediately last platoon of Somerset L.I. (detailed instructions contained in Bde Op. Orders. para. B. have been given to Lt. Lafferty, who commands the Company.

7. As D Coy. vacate their trenches in SHUTTLE LANE B Coy. will move up and take their place.

8. **METHOD of ATTACK.**
   (a) 4th Middlesex Regt. on right and 8th Somerset L.I. on left will capture first objective.
   (b) 10th Y. & L. Regt. on right and 8th LINCOLNS on left will capture second objective, passing through leading Bn.

9. (a) Time of leaving assembly trenches for 10th Y.& L. Regt. and 8th Lincolns will be given from Bde H.Qrs.
   (b) On leaving assembly trenches formation of 8th Lincolns as under.

```
            (  ─────────────────────────  )
            (         100 yds.            )
            (  ─────────────────────────  )
   B Coy. ( ─────────── 100 yds. ───────── ) A Coy.
            (  ─────────────────────────  )
            (         100 yds.            )
            (  ─────────────────────────  )
                      100 yds.

            (  ─────────────────────────  )
   C Coy. ( ─────────── 100 yds. ───────── )
            (  ─────────────────────────  )
                      100 yds.
       Bn. H.Q.  ─────────────────────   Orderlies & Signallers.
                      100 yds.
                 ─────────────────────   Battn. Grenadiers.
                      100 yrd.
                 ─────────────────────   Battn. Grenadiers.
                      100
                 ─────────────────────   R.Grend. & Stretcher Brs.
                      100 yds.
            (    D. Company   100 yds.    )
                 2    Stokes Guns.
```

D. Coy.
Advance immediately behind 8/Somersets. T
Clear out German Front line Trenches.
Forming up again in Rear of the Batt? (8 Lincs)
as shown on completing this work. R.H.T.

9. Battn. will advance in this formation, and continue their advance through the 8th Somerset L.I. without checking.

10. BARRAGES. The times of lifting for each barrage must be carefully studied and explained to all ranks, so that when the advance is ordered it can be carried straight through without having to check
All barrages must be followed up as closely as possible by the leading line of infantry.

11. On finishing work of clearing trenches D Coy. will assemble in LONELY TRENCH and LOZENGE TRENCH where he will await the arrival of the Bn., following it in rear of last line, or if Bn. has already passed before he has completed his task, he will follow on in rear until he has joined them

12. DIRECTION. The dividing line between 10th Y.& L and 8th Lincolns to 2nd objective will be X.28.a.5005 - RAILWAY COPSE. (inclusive to York & Lancs. Regt) RAILWAY to point where it enters BOTTOM WOOD X 29 a.5065.
The dividing line between 8th Lincolns and 15th D.L.I. (64th Bde.) will be X 27 b.7841 South end of SHELTER WOOD (exclusive to 8th Lincoln Regt). X 23 c.4.5 exclusive.
The left of A Coy. will direct and take the following points to march on
    Centre of LOZENGE WOOD
    50 yds. to right of CRUCIFIX
    50 yds. to left of junction of BOTTOM WOOD
    with hedgerow X 28.B 9.9.
    left of QUADRANGLE WOOD
A and B Coys. will pause on line of TRENCH TRAMWAY N.W. of RAILWAY COPSE, long enough only to straighten the line, and will advance from there to hedgerow running N.W. from BOTTOM WOOD and trench in BOTTOM WOOD. B Coy. working forward to gain trench running from BOTTOM WOOD to QUADRANGLE TRENCH as soon as possible.
Bombing parties should be sent up this trench from A Coy. as soon as they gain the bit in BOTTOM WOOD.
O.C. B Coy. will tell off an Officer and a few men to look out for advance of 15th D.L.I. on our left, and keep touch with them. 2/Lt. BAILDON 15th.D.LI. is liasion Officer 15 D.LI., and has instructions to keep touch with B Coy.
A bunch of red flowers or red material will be worn behind the neck by the directing man of each line.
C Coy. will extend the line to the right of A Coy. after passing the POODLES. They will march by their right taking the following points to march on
    East end of LOZENGE WOOD
    Right tree of POODLES
    N.W. corner of RAILWAY COPSE
    RAILWAY LINE from RAILWAY COPSE to point where it
        enters BOTTOM WOOD.

C Coy. will send forward first one platoon with its right resting on these points, and this will be their directing flank. As the gap between this platoon and A Coy. increases, other platoons must be sent up to fill it in.

They will first gain the trench running through W. end of BOTTOM WOOD down to RAILWAY; after which the right must push forward covered by fire from the left and gain the Southern edge of BOTTOM WOOD.

Parties on the right must keep touch with the Y.& L Regt. and as they advance C Coy. must push forward through the WOOD, and gain the northern edge from the N.W. corner to point X 29 A 5.6½, which line they will consolidate.

O.C. Coy. must decide whether to dig trench just inside the wood or outside.

13. When C Coy. has gained the N. edge of BOTTOM WOOD and 15 D.L.I. have gained QUADRANGLE TRENCH, which is our main objective, A & B Coys. will push forward parties to gain and consolidate our advanced objective.
(i.e) Point X 23 D 8. 1½.
QUADRANGLE WOOD, to bend in trench at X 23 D.o.5. covering the digging of the advanced trench effectively by small parties in front.

14. FLANKS. 8th Lincolnshire Regt. will take steps to safeguard their left flank, should advance of 63rd Bde be more rapid than 64th Bde.

15. COMMUNICATION TRENCHES.   UP   LINDUM ST.
                                          HUNTLEY ST.

                                  DOWN   KINGS AV,
                                            QUEENS AV.
                                            STONEHAVEN

16. STOKES MORTARS.   Two Stokes Mortars will accompany Bn. behind rear Coy.

17. STRONG POINTS.   Responsibility of garrisoning strong and supporting points is as follows :- 8 Linc. R.
    Post 18 in bend of trench at X 23 D 0 5
    Post 17 in   QUADRANGLE WOOD
    Posts 13 & 14 in N.W. end of BOTTOM WOOD

18. Each of these when completed must be garrisoned by 1 Platoon and one Lewis Gun. 8th Lincolns.
    18 by B Coy.,   17 by A Coy.
    13 by C Coy.,   14 by D Coy.

2 Vickers Guns will come up to Post 18, and 2 Vickers Guns to Post 17; probably also one or two Guns to 13 or 14, and one or two to 16 in N.E. corner of BOTTOM WOOD (this is outside our area).

19. BATTALION HEADQUARTERS. After commencement of operations Bn. H.Q. will be established at the following points.
  (a) X 27 C 4.9.
  (b) X 27 B 2.0
  (c) X 28 A 2.3
  (d) X 28 B 1.3.

20. There will be four relay stations for bringing up :-
  (a) Bombs.
  (b) Lewis Gun Magazines.
  (c) S.A.A.
from SUNKEN ROAD
They will be at SUNKEN ROAD (1)
  (2) 28 A.3.3. where road crosses trench.
  (3) 28 B.1.3
  (4) Half way up west edge of BOTTOM WOOD.
2/Lt. Duff is in charge of these relay Posts.
He will accompany carrying party of 400 men from 62nd Bde. to SUNKEN ROAD and forward (a) Ammunition.
          (b) Bombs &
          (c) Magazines ready filled.

21. EQUIPMENT. Infantry will not carry packs. Haversacks, Waterbottle, Water-proof sheet will be carried, also 220 rds. of S.A.A., 2 Grenades per man, two sandbags. Gas helmets will be worn rolled up on head.

22. TOOLS. 150 picks and 150 shovels will be equally divided among Coys. and carried as explained to Company Officers

23. FLARES. 500 flares will be distributed at VILLE.

24. COMPASS BEARING. True Bearing of line of advance of left of A Coy. as far as CRUCIFIX is 80°
From here to QUADRANGLE WOOD true bearing is 70°.
The variation of compass must be added to this to give compass bearing.

25. REGIMENTAL AID POST. Will be at junction
  MARISCHAL ST. and STONEHAVEN

26. BN. RESERVE OF AMMUNITION & BOMBS. 20 boxes S.A.A. are dumped in MARISCHAL ST. N. of HUNTLEY ST. and 1000 Bombs in MARISCHALL ST. S. of HUNTLEY STREET.
 This is the Bn. reserve which must be carried by us equally distributed among Companies.

Each Company will send an Officer and some men to draw their 5 boxes S.A.A. and 20 boxes of Bombs from these Dumps as soon as they arrive in the trenches.

This is additional to the 220 rounds S.A.A. per man, and additional to the 2 bombs per man to be carried.

This S.A.A. should be taken out of the boxes and carried slung in the bandoliers.

27. ARTILLERY. Coloured Artillery Boards should not be removed as this is a signal to the German Artillery that these trenches are in our hands.

28. ENEMY BATTERIES. Several enemy batteries have been located 200 to 300 yds. W.N.W. of BOTTOM WOOD, and there are others E. of BOTTOM WOOD.

29. OFFICER'S EQUIPMENT. All Officers will carry rifle and bayonet and revolvers, and will wear clothes as far as possible like the men. Badge of rank will be worn on the shoulder.

30. WATCHES. Watches must be set just before Bn. leaves VILLE.

31. VERY PISTOLS. All Bn. Very Pistols and Very Pistol Ammunition will be carried by Orderlies and Signallers with Bn. H. Q. and will be sent up to the Coys at night.

Orderlies going on messages should hand over Very Pistols and Very Pistol ammunition to other remaining Orderlies at Bn. H.Q.

32. STRENGTH. Bn. will go into action as strong as possible. Major Pattinson will make a nominal roll of all men who will not go into action as soon as possible.

33. SIGNALLERS. Will wear blue and white bands to enable them to lay wire in trenches without interference.

34. COMMUNICATION. Communication by Runners must be established between C. A. & B. Coys. as soon as main objective is reached, and visual signalling communication from each Coy. H.Q. to Bn. H.Q. will be made effective as quickly as possible.

H. Brown Capt. Adjt.
8th Lincolnshire Regt.

63rd Brigade. Appendix X

copy

In reply to your No 6783 of 4th July.
"D" Company was detailed to advance behind 8th Somersets & clear out German trenches. This they did. B Company coming up into position in their place.
The advance of the remainder of Battn was timed to start at 8-30 am. At 8.20 am I received message from Brigade not to start till ordered.
I was unable to stop the leading platoons of A & B Coys in time. The remainder I stopped; & telephoned to Brigade for instructions. Receiving Orders to advance with the Battn I started the remainder of the leading Coys & got messages back to our rear line on MARISCHAL Street.
The advance was progressing on the left
I advanced to point X 27 c 49. There was a good deal of Rifle & Machine gun fire here. There were some men of all Battns in 63rd Brigade & of 2 Battns of 64th Brigade. I sent parties down DART LANE to the right with bombing squad. And strung out the rest to the left along BRANDY Trench, telling them to get up to the Sunken Road.
Men were meantime getting forward up LOZENGE ALLEY, up which I advanced trying to find out the situation on the right.
I could not see any advance here. It was therefore necessary to watch our Right Flank. I pushed up men to Lozenge Wood and along Sunken Road, getting touch with 64th Brigade on Sunken Road, & in left (NORTH) portion of CRUCIFIX Trench. Those advancing up Lozenge alley meeting Germans coming from FRICOURT Farm. The Germans made 2 bombing attacks up LONELY TRENCH. both of which were repulsed. Though at one time the Germans got a few men into LOZENGE ALLEY here. They used Rifle grenades as well as bombs and so could out distance our bombers until we got up Rifle grenades. The Germans left

at least 20 dead in LONELY TRENCH close up to
LOZENGE ALLEY & some in LOZENGE ALLEY.
I asked also for Stokes guns to repel these bombing attacks
but all were out of action until later, when we got
four Stokes guns to help us, but the bombing attacks
were not repeated.
We then received orders to hold the trenches we were
in; & consolidated LOZENGE ALLEY as our Right Flank with
bombing posts up LONELY Trench & LOZENGE ALLEY &
joining up with 64th Brigade along Sunken Road.
During the night our Artillery Barrage prevented any
counter attack from Fricourt Wood.
In the morning our patrols reconnoitred LONELY TRENCH
to RED COTTAGE and LOZENGE ALLEY to FRICOURT FARM.
and found all clear.
We saw the attack advance through FRICOURT wood &
occupy FRICOURT FARM & CRUCIFIX Trench
As our Right Flank was then secure, prepared LOZENGE ALLY
for Defence facing North in case of emergency owing to the
firing we heard between between LA BOISELLE & SAUSAGE REDOBDT.
This trench was made quite strong, being worked on until
we got orders to move – meantime we had to pass
up all our S.A.A. reserve, Rifle Grenades & STOKES Mortar
ammunition to the 62nd Brigade & our hand grenades & a
squad of bombers were sent up to 62nd Brigade together
with supplies from the Rear.
We then received orders to move to PATCH ALLEY
facing north with our Right on Sunken Road. Arriving
there we continued work of preparing the trench
for defence; until we were relieved about 2 am
on the 4th, when we marched to DERNACOURT.

Vaux
5. 7. 16.

(Sd) R. H. Johnston Lt. Col.
Commdg 8th Bn Lincolnshire Regt

From: M.O. 8/Lincoln Regt.
To: A.D.M.S. 21st Division.

COPY (Y)

I have the honour to submit this report of the operations carried out at my R.A.P. from June 30th to July 3rd 1916.

I moved into the Stonehaven St dug-out just before midnight on June 30th, bringing in final stores and preparing to receive cases.

The 10 bearers from the 65th F. Amb mentioned in your operation orders, not having shown up by 1.0 am, I sent a guide down to the A.D.S. to bring them up. Instead of bearers he brought a verbal message that they would come "early in the morning."

Work started about 2.0 am and soon increased in the rate of cases, till about 6.0 am I had to start sending down stretchers by regimental bearers. I sent a written message to O.C. 65th F. Amb when I thought that the time specified as "early in the morning" had more than arrived.

This and another message sent to the A.D.M.S. evoked no response in bearers or otherwise.

Up to about 12 noon I had dressed & evacuated about 100 cases, giving anti-t.S. when there was time and providing tea etc before sending them down.

About mid-day the M.O. of a battalion in the 62nd Brigade arrived and said that he wished to take over the Stonehaven St dug-out.

As it was showing signs of filling up with stretchers with no one to carry them, I handed it over and leaving the more important stores under the charge of the chaplain and an orderly a little further up Stonehaven St, crossed into the German trenches.

I found No Man's land still swept by Machine Guns and receiving a mild barrage from field guns.

As this was unsuitable for the passage of stretchers, I returned to Stonehaven St, and for about an hour carried on in the trench.

Then, as things were quieter in front, I transferred my R.A.P. to a M.G. emplacement in the German front trench, where there was fair cover. The German dug-outs are useless for the purpose, as the entrances are very steep and deep and stretcher cases could not be got into them.

By now nearly all my bearers had gone back to Becourt with cases, so that I applied dressings and evacuated as quickly as possible using my observer, messengers and other odd orderlies as bearers.

Later I found the 1st Bn Lincolnshire Regt's bearers who had lost their M.O. and with their help carried on the R.A.P. at full pressure till the morning of 2nd.

The First Lines bearers then rejoined their M.O. on the Sunken road.

My Battalion was by now in reserve and not likely to move over the Sunken road which was only 600 yards in advance of my position.

Accordingly I remained in the M.G. emplacement till the Division moved out July 4th.

On the 2nd & 3rd I received most valuable

assistance from a party of R.A.M.C. bearers kindly lent to me by the 53rd F. Amb.

These men worked very hard and intelligently till I dismissed them on the night of 3rd when work was almost over as far as we were concerned.

The only bearers from our own Ambulances that I saw were a party of six with two stretchers belonging to the 64th F. Amb. I had one case in at the time and instructed three of them to take him down and the other three to wait for another who was then being brought in. Unfortunately I turned my back for a moment and the second three dumped their stretcher and walked back to Queen's Redt with the others.

The outstanding feature of the operation was as before the failure of the Field Ambulances to get in touch with us.

If I could have had ten reliable bearers as promised, a large number of wounded would have been saved many hours of exposure.

As it was, all were evacuated in time, though many had to walk down who should have been carried.

The casualties among my bearers and orderlies were one man bruised.

Attached is a list of wounded of other Units evacuated by me. Some minor cases escaped tabulation in the busiest time.

(Sd) A. Douglas Smart, Capt R.A.M.C.

5-7-17.

www.ingramcontent.com/pod-product-compliance
Lightning Source LLC
Chambersburg PA
CBHW081238170426

43191CB00034B/1965